Logan Gray

Beyond Beliefs
The Philosophy of Agnosticism

Copyright
Original Title: Beyond Beliefs: The Philosophy of Agnosticism
Copyright: © 2024 Luiz Antonio dos Santos
All rights reserved.
Publisher: Booklas / Luiz Antonio dos Santos
Address: José Delalíbera, street 962
86.183-550 – Cambé – PR
Contact: suporte@booklas.com
Website: www.booklas.com

Credits:
Author: Logan Gray
Editor: Luiz Antonio dos Santos
Proofreading: Ana Maria Ferreira
Graphic Design and Layout: Pedro Henrique Oliveira
Cover Design: Sofia Almeida

Classification:
Categories: Philosophy, Epistemology, Agnosticism, History of Thought.
DDC: 128.1 - UDC: 101 -

Note:
This book addresses the foundations of agnosticism, exploring its philosophical, historical, and epistemological roots. It is intended for those seeking a deep and critical reflection on the nature of knowledge, belief, and uncertainty. The information presented here promotes intellectual self-awareness and is not intended to replace professional guidance in other fields.

The total or partial reproduction of this work by any means or process is prohibited without prior authorization from the copyright holder.

Summary

Prologue 5
Chapter 1 Defining Agnosticism 8
Chapter 2 Types of Agnosticism 11
Chapter 3 Skepticism versus Agnosticism 15
Chapter 4 Historical Origins 18
Chapter 5 Huxley and Agnosticism 22
Chapter 6 Context of the 19th Century 25
Chapter 7 Darwin and Evolution 29
Chapter 8 Agnosticism and Religion 33
Chapter 9 Atheism and Agnosticism 36
Chapter 10 Deism and Agnosticism 39
Chapter 11 Pantheism and Agnosticism 42
Chapter 12 Gnosticism and Agnosticism 45
Chapter 13 Epistemological Questions 48
Chapter 14 Limits of Certainty 51
Chapter 15 Evidence and Belief 54
Chapter 16 Burden of Proof 58
Chapter 17 Cosmological Arguments 61
Chapter 18 Teleological Arguments 64
Chapter 19 The Ontological Argument 68
Chapter 20 The Problem of Evil 71
Chapter 21 Religious Experience 74
Chapter 22 Faith and Reason 77
Chapter 23 Morality and Agnosticism 80

Chapter 24 Secular Humanism 83
Chapter 25 Existentialism and Agnosticism 86
Chapter 26 Free Will 89
Chapter 27 Consciousness and the Soul 92
Chapter 28 Life After Death 95
Chapter 29 Science and Agnosticism 98
Chapter 30 Naturalism 101
Chapter 31 Materialism 104
Chapter 32 Reductionism 107
Chapter 33 Emergentism 110
Chapter 34 Chaos and Complexity 113
Chapter 35 The Universe in Evolution 117
Chapter 36 Origin of Life 120
Chapter 37 Human Evolution 123
Chapter 38 Artificial Intelligence 126
Chapter 39 The Future of Humanity 129
Chapter 40 Agnosticism and Society 132
Chapter 41 Secularism 135
Chapter 42 Religious Tolerance 139
Chapter 43 Freedom of Expression 142
Chapter 44 Critical Thinking 145
Chapter 45 Scientific Skepticism 148
Chapter 46 Logical Fallacie 152
Chapter 47 The Scientific Method 156
Chapter 48 Rationality 160
Chapter 49 Emotions and Reason 163
Chapter 50 Cognitive Biases 166

Chapter 51 The Agnostic Community 170
Chapter 52 Resources for Agnostics 173
Chapter 53 Living as an Agnostic 177
Chapter 54 Finding Meaning 180
Chapter 55 Celebrating Life 183
Chapter 56 The Future of Agnosticism 186
Epilogue 189

Prologue

Your choice to stand before this book is no accident; it is the point of convergence between what you seek and what, perhaps unknowingly, has already begun shaping your deepest doubts. This text does not aim to impose certainties or offer ready-made paths. On the contrary, it proposes an intellectual challenge: to face the vastness of the unknown with courage and clarity.

We live in an age of easy answers and hasty definitions. Knowledge is often treated as a product to be consumed, something to reassure us and confirm our most comfortable beliefs. But there is another kind of knowledge—rarer, more unsettling, and infinitely more valuable. It is the knowledge that accepts the limits of what we can comprehend while refusing complacent ignorance. This is the knowledge that awaits you in the following pages.

Agnosticism. A word that, for many, is just a label or a middle-ground position. For others, however, it is the most sophisticated of philosophical stances. Not because it sits on the fence, but because it recognizes the depth of the abyss separating what we know from what we may never know. Here, you will be challenged to explore that gap, to see knowledge not as a fortress of certainties but as an ever-expanding horizon.

This book is not for those who seek simple answers. It demands from you a willingness to face discomfort, to abandon comfortable truths, and to question the foundations of your most deeply held beliefs. Why do we believe what we believe? What defines what we claim to know? And, more importantly, what does it mean not to know?

The proposition is clear: discard dogmas, embrace doubt, and acknowledge that intellectual humility is the only stance compatible with the complexity of the universe. This is an invitation to free yourself from the trenches of theism and atheism and enter a territory where questions matter more than answers. A territory where intellectual honesty is not merely an ideal but a daily practice.

Throughout these pages, you will encounter ideas that will deconstruct established notions and reshape your paradigms. The origin of the term agnostic, Huxley's vision, the philosophical and scientific implications—all of these will be explored with the depth that such questions demand. More than a philosophy, what you hold in your hands is a methodology, a way of thinking that rejects superficiality and embraces rigor.

It is possible that, by the end of this book, you will not have definitive answers. And that is intentional. The greatness of agnosticism lies precisely in its refusal to accept definitive answers to questions that surpass the limits of reason and evidence. It is not about resignation but about a profound respect for the complexity of the world and our limited capacity to fully understand it.

So, what will you do? Will you remain on the surface, where everything is predictable and safe, or will you dare to explore the depths of uncertainty? The choice is yours, but one thing is certain: the journey this book proposes is for those unafraid to think, those who are not satisfied with what is easy, and those who understand that true knowledge begins when we admit how much we have yet to learn.

Welcome to the challenge. Here, truth is not a destination but the journey itself.

Chapter 1
Defining Agnosticism

Agnosticism, at its core, is a philosophical stance that revolves around the knowability of certain claims, most often those related to the existence or nature of deities or the divine. It's a nuanced position that often gets simplified or misconstrued in popular discourse. This chapter delves deep into the definition of agnosticism, exploring its etymological roots, dissecting its various interpretations, and distinguishing it from closely related concepts like atheism and skepticism.

Etymology and Core Concept:

The term "agnosticism" has its roots in the Greek word "agnostos," meaning "unknowable" or "not known." This etymology provides a fundamental understanding of the term: agnostics assert that certain things, particularly those concerning the supernatural or the ultimate nature of reality, are beyond the scope of human knowledge.

It's crucial to remember that agnosticism is not simply about deities. While the existence of God is a central question in many agnostic discussions, the philosophy extends to any claim that is considered inherently unknowable. This could include questions about the afterlife, the soul, or even the true nature of consciousness.

The Spectrum of Agnostic Thought:

Agnosticism isn't a monolithic concept. It encompasses a spectrum of views, each with subtle but significant differences. Here are some of the key distinctions:

Strong Agnosticism: This position asserts that the existence or nature of God is ultimately unknowable by any means. It suggests an inherent limitation to human knowledge when it comes to metaphysical questions. Strong agnostics believe that no amount of evidence or reasoning can definitively prove or disprove such claims.

Weak Agnosticism: This perspective acknowledges the current lack of sufficient evidence to prove or disprove the existence of God but leaves open the possibility that future evidence or advancements in understanding might change that. Weak agnostics essentially say, "I don't know now, but I might be able to know in the future."

Apathetic Agnosticism: This variant focuses on the practical implications of not knowing. Apathetic agnostics argue that since the existence of God is unknowable, it's irrelevant to their lives and decisions. They may see the pursuit of such knowledge as futile or unimportant.

Implicit Agnosticism: This refers to the inherent agnosticism present in many philosophical and scientific positions. For instance, a scientist focusing solely on the natural world might be implicitly agnostic about supernatural claims, not because they actively deny them, but because they fall outside the scope of their investigations.

Distinguishing Agnosticism from Related Concepts:

Agnosticism is often confused with other philosophical stances, particularly atheism and skepticism. While there are overlaps, it's important to understand the key distinctions:

Agnosticism vs. Atheism: Atheism is the disbelief in the existence of God. While some agnostics may also be atheists, the two are not synonymous. An agnostic might say, "I don't know if God exists," while an atheist would say, "I don't believe God exists." The key difference lies in the degree of certainty. Agnosticism focuses on the lack of knowledge, while atheism expresses a definite lack of belief.

Agnosticism vs. Skepticism: Skepticism is a broader philosophical approach that questions the possibility of certain knowledge. While agnostics are often skeptical about specific claims, particularly those related to the supernatural, skepticism can apply to a wider range of beliefs. A skeptic might question the reliability of our senses or the validity of certain scientific theories. Agnosticism can be seen as a specific form of skepticism focused on metaphysical claims.

Agnosticism as a Middle Ground:

Agnosticism often occupies a middle ground between theism and atheism. It avoids the definitive claims of both, acknowledging the limitations of human knowledge and understanding. This position can be seen as intellectually humble, recognizing that there are questions that may forever remain beyond our grasp.

The Importance of Context:

The meaning and implications of agnosticism can vary depending on the context. For example, in a religious debate, an agnostic might emphasize the lack of definitive proof for the existence of God. In a scientific context, agnosticism might refer to the limitations of current knowledge about the universe. It's essential to consider the specific context when interpreting the meaning of agnosticism.

Agnosticism is a complex and multifaceted philosophical stance. It's not merely a lack of belief in God but a nuanced position that acknowledges the limitations of human knowledge when it comes to certain claims, particularly those concerning the supernatural. Understanding the different types of agnosticism and its relationship to other philosophical concepts is crucial for engaging in meaningful discussions about knowledge, belief, and the nature of reality.

Chapter 2
Types of Agnosticism

In the previous chapter, we established that agnosticism is not a singular, rigid concept. Instead, it encompasses a spectrum of viewpoints, each with its own nuances and implications. This chapter dives deeper into these diverse types of agnosticism, exploring their subtle differences and how they manifest in various contexts. Understanding these variations is crucial for grasping the full scope and complexity of agnostic thought.

1. Strong Agnosticism:

Strong agnosticism, also known as hard agnosticism or permanent agnosticism, represents a firm conviction that the existence or nature of God, and perhaps other metaphysical claims, are inherently unknowable by human beings. It posits a fundamental limitation to our cognitive abilities, suggesting that no amount of evidence, reasoning, or experience can ever definitively resolve these questions.

Key Characteristics:

Unknowability: Strong agnostics emphasize the inherent unknowability of certain propositions, particularly those related to the divine. They believe these questions lie beyond the realm of human comprehension, much like a dog might struggle to grasp advanced calculus.

Permanence: This stance implies that the unknowability is not a temporary limitation due to current lack of evidence or understanding. It's a permanent epistemological barrier, suggesting that even with future advancements, these questions will remain forever unanswered.

Certainty about Unknowability: While acknowledging the lack of knowledge about the divine, strong agnostics express a strong conviction about the impossibility of ever attaining such knowledge. This certainty about the unknowability itself is a defining feature of this position.

2. Weak Agnosticism:

Weak agnosticism, also referred to as soft agnosticism or empirical agnosticism, adopts a more open-ended approach. It acknowledges the current lack of sufficient evidence to prove or disprove the existence of God or other metaphysical claims but doesn't rule out the possibility of future discoveries or advancements that could change this.

Key Characteristics:

Provisional Nature: Weak agnostics hold their position provisionally. They acknowledge the limitations of current knowledge but remain open to the possibility of future evidence or arguments swaying their perspective.

Emphasis on Evidence: This type of agnosticism places a high value on empirical evidence and rational inquiry. Weak agnostics are willing to revise their position if presented with compelling evidence or arguments.

Potential for Knowledge: Unlike strong agnosticism, this view doesn't assume an inherent limitation to human knowledge. It suggests that while we may not know now, we might be able to know in the future.

3. Apathetic Agnosticism:

Apathetic agnosticism, sometimes called pragmatic agnosticism, shifts the focus from the question of knowability to the practical implications of not knowing. Apathetic agnostics argue that since the existence of God or other metaphysical realities is ultimately unknowable, it's irrelevant to their lives and decisions.

Key Characteristics:

Focus on Practicality: This perspective prioritizes practical concerns over theoretical debates. Apathetic agnostics may see metaphysical inquiries as futile or unproductive, choosing to focus on matters that have a tangible impact on their lives.

Indifference to the Unknowable: They don't necessarily deny the possibility of God or other metaphysical realities, but they remain indifferent to these questions. They might argue that these issues have no bearing on how they live their lives or make moral choices.

Emphasis on This-Worldly Concerns: Apathetic agnostics tend to focus on issues related to this world, such as social justice, environmental protection, or personal well-being, rather than pondering unanswerable questions about the supernatural.

4. Implicit Agnosticism:

Implicit agnosticism is not a self-consciously adopted position but rather an inherent aspect of certain approaches to knowledge and inquiry. It's often found in scientific and philosophical frameworks that limit their investigations to the natural world, effectively bracketing out supernatural or metaphysical claims.

Key Characteristics:

Focus on the Natural World: Scientists, for instance, often adopt an implicitly agnostic stance by focusing solely on natural phenomena and explanations. This doesn't necessarily imply a denial of the supernatural, but rather a methodological choice to limit their investigations to the observable and testable.

Suspension of Judgment on Metaphysical Claims: Implicit agnostics may not actively engage in debates about the existence of God or other metaphysical realities. They may simply suspend judgment on these issues, considering them outside the scope of their inquiry.

Not Necessarily a Philosophical Position: Implicit agnosticism is more of a practical approach to knowledge than a consciously held philosophical stance. It reflects a focus on what can be known and investigated through empirical observation and rational inquiry.

5. Other Variations:

Beyond these main types, other variations and combinations of agnosticism exist. Some individuals might identify as agnostic atheists, expressing both a lack of belief in God and an acknowledgment of the unknowability of the divine. Others might adopt a more spiritual form of agnosticism, remaining open to the possibility of a transcendent reality while acknowledging the limitations of human understanding.

The Importance of Recognizing Diversity:

Understanding the diverse types of agnosticism is crucial for avoiding misunderstandings and stereotypes. It's essential to recognize that agnostics don't all hold the same views or approach questions of knowledge and belief in the same way. This diversity enriches the agnostic perspective and allows for a more nuanced understanding of the complex relationship between knowledge, belief, and the unknown.

Agnosticism is a multifaceted philosophical stance that encompasses a spectrum of viewpoints, each with its own unique characteristics and implications. By understanding the different types of agnosticism, we can appreciate the full scope and complexity of this approach to knowledge and belief. Whether one adopts a strong, weak, apathetic, or implicit form of agnosticism, the core principle remains the same: an acknowledgment of the limitations of human knowledge, particularly when it comes to questions about the ultimate nature of reality and the existence of the divine.

Chapter 3
Skepticism versus Agnosticism

Agnosticism and skepticism are closely related philosophical concepts that often get intertwined and even used interchangeably. Both involve questioning knowledge claims and acknowledging limitations in human understanding. However, they are distinct perspectives with unique focuses and implications. This chapter aims to disentangle these two concepts, exploring their similarities, differences, and how they relate to each other in the broader landscape of philosophical inquiry.

Skepticism: A Broad Epistemological Approach:

Skepticism, in its most general form, is an approach to knowledge that emphasizes doubt and questioning. It challenges the certainty of our beliefs and encourages critical examination of the evidence and reasoning behind them. Skepticism can be applied to a wide range of knowledge claims, from everyday observations to scientific theories and religious doctrines.

Key Characteristics of Skepticism:

Doubt as a Starting Point: Skeptics often begin with a position of doubt, questioning the validity and reliability of our sources of knowledge, including our senses, reasoning, and testimony from others.

Critical Inquiry: Skepticism promotes critical thinking and the rigorous evaluation of evidence. It encourages us to look for potential flaws in our reasoning, biases that might distort our perceptions, and alternative explanations for phenomena.

Suspension of Judgment: In some cases, skeptics may suspend judgment on certain claims, acknowledging the limitations of current knowledge and the possibility of future discoveries that could change our understanding.

Varying Degrees of Skepticism: Skepticism exists on a spectrum, from moderate skepticism, which questions specific claims or types of knowledge, to radical skepticism, which doubts the possibility of any certain knowledge at all.

Agnosticism: A Focused Form of Skepticism:

Agnosticism can be seen as a specific application of skepticism, primarily focused on metaphysical claims, particularly those related to the existence or nature of God, the afterlife, and the soul. While skepticism casts a wider net, questioning the possibility of knowledge in various domains, agnosticism hones in on the knowability of specific types of claims that often lie beyond the realm of empirical investigation.

Key Characteristics of Agnosticism in Relation to Skepticism:

Specificity: Agnosticism targets specific types of knowledge claims, primarily those related to the supernatural or the ultimate nature of reality. It doesn't necessarily question the validity of knowledge in other areas, such as scientific or historical knowledge.

Emphasis on the Unknowable: Agnostics assert that certain claims, particularly those related to the divine, are inherently unknowable, either due to the limitations of human cognition or the nature of the claims themselves.

Relationship to Evidence: Agnostics often base their position on the lack of sufficient evidence to support or refute metaphysical claims. They may argue that the available evidence is inconclusive or that the nature of these claims makes them impervious to empirical investigation.

Similarities between Skepticism and Agnosticism:

Questioning Knowledge Claims: Both skepticism and agnosticism involve questioning the certainty of knowledge claims and acknowledging the potential for error and bias in our understanding.

Emphasis on Critical Thinking: Both perspectives promote critical thinking and the careful evaluation of evidence before accepting claims as true.

Humility in the Face of the Unknown: Both skeptics and agnostics demonstrate a degree of intellectual humility, recognizing the limitations of human knowledge and the vastness of the unknown.

Differences between Skepticism and Agnosticism:

Scope: Skepticism is a broader epistemological approach that can be applied to a wide range of knowledge claims, while agnosticism focuses specifically on the knowability of metaphysical claims.

Focus: Skepticism emphasizes doubt and questioning as a general approach to knowledge, while agnosticism focuses on the limitations of human knowledge in specific domains.

Implications: Skepticism can lead to a more cautious and questioning approach to all knowledge claims, while agnosticism primarily affects one's beliefs about the supernatural and the ultimate nature of reality.

Examples of Skepticism and Agnosticism in Action:

Skepticism: A skeptic might question the reliability of eyewitness testimony in a court case, or they might critically evaluate the claims of a scientific study before accepting its conclusions.

Agnosticism: An agnostic might argue that the existence of God is unknowable due to the lack of empirical evidence or the inherent limitations of human understanding.

Skepticism and agnosticism are valuable philosophical tools for navigating the complexities of knowledge and belief. While skepticism provides a broad framework for critical inquiry, agnosticism offers a focused lens for examining specific types of claims, particularly those related to the supernatural. By understanding the nuances of these two perspectives, we can develop a more nuanced and sophisticated approach to knowledge, recognizing both the potential and the limitations of human understanding.

Chapter 4
Historical Origins

While the term "agnosticism" was coined in the 19th century, the underlying philosophical ideas and inquiries that characterize it have a long and rich history, stretching back to ancient civilizations. This chapter delves into the historical origins of agnostic thought, exploring its precursors in ancient Greece, India, and other cultures. By examining these early expressions of doubt and questioning, we can gain a deeper appreciation for the enduring relevance of agnosticism and its place in the evolution of human thought.

Ancient Greece: Seeds of Agnostic Thought:

Ancient Greece, a cradle of Western philosophy, witnessed the emergence of ideas that resonate with modern agnosticism. Several prominent thinkers expressed skepticism about the existence of gods or the possibility of attaining certain knowledge about the divine.

Protagoras (c. 490 – c. 420 BCE): Often considered the first major Sophist, Protagoras famously declared, "Man is the measure of all things: of things which are, that they are, and of things which are not, that they are not." This relativistic view suggests that truth and knowledge are subjective and dependent on individual perception, casting doubt on the possibility of objective knowledge about the divine. Protagoras's agnostic leanings are further evident in his statement, "Concerning the gods, I have no means of knowing whether they exist or not or of what sort they may be, because of the obscurity of the subject, and the brevity of human life."

Socrates (c. 470 – 399 BCE): While not explicitly an agnostic, Socrates's method of inquiry, based on questioning and challenging assumptions, laid the groundwork for skeptical and agnostic thought. His famous dictum, "The only true wisdom is in knowing you know nothing," reflects a humility about the limits of human knowledge that resonates with agnostic perspectives.

Pyrrho of Elis (c. 360 – c. 270 BCE): The founder of Pyrrhonian skepticism, Pyrrho advocated for the suspension of judgment on all matters, including the existence of gods. He argued that since we cannot attain certain knowledge, it's best to withhold belief and avoid making definitive claims about the nature of reality.

Ancient India: Questioning the Vedas:
Ancient Indian philosophy also grappled with questions about the nature of reality and the existence of the divine. Several schools of thought expressed skepticism about the authority of the Vedas, the sacred texts of Hinduism, and the possibility of attaining knowledge about the ultimate reality.

Ajñana (Non-knowledge): The concept of Ajñana, meaning "non-knowledge" or "ignorance," played a significant role in various Indian philosophical traditions. It refers to the inherent limitations of human understanding and the impossibility of grasping the ultimate reality through ordinary means.

Nāstika (Heterodox) Schools: Several heterodox schools of Indian philosophy, such as Jainism and Buddhism, challenged the authority of the Vedas and the traditional Hindu worldview. While not strictly agnostic, they questioned the existence of a creator god and emphasized the importance of empirical observation and critical inquiry.

Cārvāka: This materialistic school of thought rejected the existence of the soul, the afterlife, and the authority of the Vedas. They advocated for a focus on the material world and the pursuit of pleasure in this life.

Other Ancient Traditions:
Agnostic tendencies can also be found in other ancient traditions, such as:

Ancient China: Philosophers like Lao Tzu and Zhuangzi expressed skepticism about the possibility of attaining absolute knowledge and emphasized the importance of living in harmony with the Dao, the natural order of the universe.

Pre-Socratic Philosophers: Thinkers like Xenophanes and Democritus questioned traditional Greek mythology and offered naturalistic explanations for phenomena previously attributed to the gods.

The Middle Ages: Seeds of Doubt Amidst Dogmatism:
While the Middle Ages in Europe were largely dominated by religious dogma, some thinkers continued to express skepticism and question the prevailing worldview.

Islamic Philosophy: Scholars like Al-Ghazali and Averroes engaged in critical analysis of religious doctrines and explored the limits of human reason.

Jewish Philosophy: Thinkers like Maimonides grappled with the relationship between faith and reason, acknowledging the limitations of human understanding while upholding the importance of religious tradition.

The Renaissance and the Reformation:
The Renaissance and the Reformation marked a period of intellectual upheaval and renewed interest in classical philosophy, paving the way for the emergence of modern skepticism and agnosticism.

Michel de Montaigne (1533-1592): A French essayist, Montaigne explored the limitations of human knowledge and the relativity of truth, expressing skepticism about the possibility of attaining certainty in any domain.

Erasmus of Rotterdam (1466-1536): A humanist scholar, Erasmus advocated for critical engagement with religious texts and questioned the authority of the Church.

The Enlightenment and the Rise of Reason:
The Enlightenment, with its emphasis on reason and empirical observation, further fueled the development of skeptical and agnostic thought.

David Hume (1711-1776): A Scottish philosopher, Hume's skeptical inquiries challenged the foundations of knowledge and cast doubt on the possibility of proving the existence of God through reason alone.

Immanuel Kant (1724-1804): A German philosopher, Kant argued that human knowledge is limited to the phenomenal world, the world of appearances, and that we cannot know the noumenal world, the world of things-in-themselves, including the existence of God.

The historical origins of agnosticism reveal a long and diverse tradition of questioning, doubt, and critical inquiry. From ancient Greece to India and beyond, thinkers have grappled with the limitations of human knowledge and the possibility of attaining certainty about the divine. By tracing these historical roots, we can gain a deeper understanding of the enduring relevance of agnosticism and its contribution to the evolution of human thought. As we continue our exploration of agnosticism, we will see how these early seeds of doubt blossomed into a more formalized philosophical stance in the modern era.

Chapter 5
Huxley and Agnosticism

While the philosophical underpinnings of agnosticism can be traced back to antiquity, it was in the 19th century that the term itself was coined and the concept gained wider recognition. This was largely due to the work of Thomas Henry Huxley, a prominent British biologist and advocate for science. This chapter delves into Huxley's pivotal role in shaping modern agnosticism, exploring his motivations, his definition of the term, and the impact of his ideas on the intellectual landscape of his time and beyond.

Huxley's Background and Intellectual Context:

Thomas Henry Huxley (1825-1895) was a leading figure in Victorian science, often referred to as "Darwin's Bulldog" for his fierce defense of evolutionary theory. He was a passionate advocate for scientific education and a vocal critic of religious dogma and superstition. His intellectual context was shaped by the rapid advancements in science and the growing tension between scientific inquiry and traditional religious beliefs.

The Coining of "Agnosticism":

In 1869, Huxley coined the term "agnostic" during a meeting of the Metaphysical Society in London. He felt that existing labels like "atheist" and "theist" did not accurately reflect his own position, which emphasized the limitations of human knowledge and the impossibility of attaining certainty about metaphysical claims. He derived the term from the Greek word "agnostos," meaning "unknowable," reflecting his conviction that certain questions, particularly those related to the existence and nature of God, were beyond the reach of human understanding.

Huxley's Definition of Agnosticism:
Huxley defined agnosticism as a principle of intellectual honesty and rigorous inquiry. He argued that it was essential to suspend judgment on matters where there was insufficient evidence and to avoid making claims that could not be substantiated. He saw agnosticism not as a definitive answer to metaphysical questions but as a method for approaching them with intellectual integrity.

Key Elements of Huxley's Agnosticism:
Emphasis on Evidence: Huxley stressed the importance of empirical evidence and scientific methodology in the pursuit of knowledge. He argued that beliefs should be based on evidence and that it was essential to remain open to revising one's views in light of new evidence.

Rejection of Dogmatism: Huxley was critical of both religious and scientific dogmatism, arguing that any claim to absolute certainty was unwarranted. He believed that knowledge was always provisional and subject to revision.

Focus on Ethical Conduct: Huxley emphasized the importance of ethical conduct and social responsibility, even in the absence of certainty about metaphysical questions. He argued that morality could be grounded in human experience and reason, without relying on religious doctrines.

Huxley's Contributions to Agnostic Thought:
Formalization of the Concept: By coining the term "agnostic" and articulating its principles, Huxley provided a framework for understanding and expressing a position that had previously lacked a clear definition.

Defense of Scientific Inquiry: Huxley's advocacy for agnosticism was intertwined with his defense of scientific inquiry and his critique of religious dogma that hindered scientific progress.

Promotion of Intellectual Honesty: Huxley's emphasis on evidence and his rejection of dogmatism helped to promote a culture of intellectual honesty and critical thinking.

Impact and Legacy:

Huxley's ideas had a significant impact on the intellectual landscape of his time and continue to resonate today. Agnosticism gained wider acceptance as a legitimate philosophical position, and Huxley's emphasis on evidence and critical thinking influenced the development of scientific skepticism and secular humanism.

Criticisms and Misinterpretations:

Huxley's agnosticism has not been without its critics. Some have argued that it is too passive and that it avoids taking a stand on important issues. Others have accused it of being a form of disguised atheism. However, Huxley himself rejected these criticisms, arguing that agnosticism was not about avoiding questions but about approaching them with intellectual honesty and rigor.

Thomas Henry Huxley played a pivotal role in shaping modern agnosticism. His coining of the term, his clear articulation of its principles, and his passionate defense of scientific inquiry helped to establish agnosticism as a respected philosophical position. His emphasis on evidence, critical thinking, and ethical conduct continues to inspire those who seek to navigate the complexities of knowledge and belief in a world where certainty is often elusive.

Chapter 6
Context of the 19th Century

The emergence of agnosticism in the 19th century cannot be understood in isolation. It was a product of its time, deeply intertwined with the social, intellectual, and cultural currents that shaped the era. This chapter explores the historical context in which agnosticism arose, examining the key factors that contributed to its development and its impact on the evolving relationship between science, religion, and philosophy.

The Rise of Science and Reason:

The 19th century witnessed unprecedented advancements in science and technology, transforming the way people understood the world. Discoveries in fields like geology, biology, and physics challenged traditional religious explanations for natural phenomena. The rise of scientific thinking, with its emphasis on empirical evidence and rational inquiry, created a fertile ground for questioning long-held beliefs and seeking naturalistic explanations for the universe and its workings.

Geological Discoveries: Geological findings, such as the discovery of fossils and the development of geological time scales, challenged the biblical account of creation and the age of the Earth. This sparked debates about the compatibility of science and religion and opened the door for alternative explanations for the origins of life and the universe.

Darwin's Theory of Evolution: Charles Darwin's theory of evolution by natural selection, published in 1859, revolutionized biology and had a profound impact on religious and philosophical thought. The idea that species evolved over time through natural processes challenged the notion of divine creation and raised questions about the place of humans in the natural world.

Advances in Physics and Astronomy: Discoveries in physics and astronomy, such as the laws of thermodynamics and the vastness of the universe, further expanded our understanding of the natural world and challenged anthropocentric views of the cosmos.

The Enlightenment Legacy:

The intellectual ferment of the 19th century was also influenced by the legacy of the Enlightenment, a philosophical movement of the 18th century that emphasized reason, individual liberty, and scientific inquiry. Enlightenment thinkers like John Locke, David Hume, and Immanuel Kant had laid the groundwork for questioning traditional authority and seeking knowledge through reason and observation.

Emphasis on Reason: The Enlightenment's emphasis on reason and critical thinking encouraged individuals to question received wisdom and seek evidence-based explanations for phenomena. This created a climate of intellectual curiosity and openness to new ideas that fostered the development of agnosticism.

Individual Liberty: The Enlightenment's emphasis on individual liberty and freedom of thought challenged the authority of religious institutions and encouraged individuals to form their own beliefs based on reason and evidence.

Scientific Progress: The Enlightenment's faith in scientific progress and the power of human reason to understand the natural world fueled the scientific revolution of the 19th century and contributed to the growing tension between science and religion.

Social and Cultural Changes:

The 19th century was a period of significant social and cultural change, marked by industrialization, urbanization, and the rise of new social classes. These changes also contributed to the rise of agnosticism by challenging traditional social structures and creating a more diverse and pluralistic society.

Industrialization and Urbanization: The Industrial Revolution led to the growth of cities and the emergence of a new urban working class. This disrupted traditional social structures and created a more fluid and dynamic society where individuals were less bound by traditional religious and social norms.

Rise of the Middle Class: The growth of the middle class, with its emphasis on education and social mobility, created a new audience for intellectual and philosophical ideas. This contributed to the spread of scientific knowledge and the growing popularity of agnostic and secular perspectives.

Social Reform Movements: The 19th century also witnessed the rise of various social reform movements, such as the abolitionist movement and the women's suffrage movement. These movements challenged traditional social hierarchies and promoted the values of equality and individual rights, which resonated with the agnostic emphasis on individual autonomy and freedom of thought.

Religious Debates and Controversies:

The 19th century was also marked by intense debates and controversies within religious circles, as different denominations and theological perspectives grappled with the challenges posed by science and modernity. These debates contributed to the rise of agnosticism by highlighting the diversity of religious beliefs and the difficulty of achieving consensus on religious matters.

Theological Liberalism: Theological liberalism, which sought to reconcile religious beliefs with modern science and philosophy, gained ground in the 19th century. This movement challenged traditional interpretations of scripture and emphasized the importance of reason and experience in religious understanding.

Biblical Criticism: The development of biblical criticism, which applied historical and literary analysis to the Bible, challenged traditional views of scripture as divinely inspired and infallible. This raised questions about the authority of religious texts and opened the door for alternative interpretations of religious doctrines.

Religious Conflicts: The 19th century also witnessed numerous religious conflicts and persecutions, highlighting the dangers of religious intolerance and the need for greater religious freedom. This further fueled the rise of agnosticism and secularism as alternatives to traditional religious beliefs.

The emergence of agnosticism in the 19th century was a complex phenomenon, shaped by a confluence of factors, including the rise of science and reason, the legacy of the Enlightenment, social and cultural changes, and religious debates and controversies. Agnosticism emerged as a response to the challenges posed by modernity, offering a way to navigate the complexities of knowledge and belief in a world where traditional certainties were being questioned. By understanding the historical context in which agnosticism arose, we can gain a deeper appreciation for its significance and its enduring relevance in the 21st century.

Chapter 7
Darwin and Evolution

Charles Darwin's theory of evolution by natural selection, arguably the most significant scientific breakthrough of the 19th century, had a profound and lasting impact on religious and philosophical thought, including the development of agnosticism. This chapter explores the intricate relationship between Darwin's ideas and the rise of agnosticism, examining how evolutionary theory challenged traditional views of creation, human origins, and the role of a divine creator.

Pre-Darwinian Views on Creation:

Before Darwin, the dominant view in Western thought was that of special creation, which held that each species was created individually and immutably by God. This view was deeply ingrained in religious doctrines and provided a framework for understanding the natural world and humanity's place within it. However, emerging scientific discoveries in fields like geology and paleontology began to challenge this traditional view, suggesting that the Earth was much older than previously thought and that species had changed over time.

Darwin's Theory of Evolution:

In 1859, Charles Darwin published his groundbreaking work, "On the Origin of Species," which presented his theory of evolution by natural selection. This theory proposed that species evolve over time through a process of natural selection, where individuals with traits better suited to their environment are more likely to survive and reproduce, passing on their advantageous traits to their offspring. This process, over vast periods of time, leads to the gradual evolution of new species.

Challenges to Traditional Beliefs:

Darwin's theory challenged several core tenets of traditional religious beliefs:

The immutability of species: Evolutionary theory directly contradicted the idea that species were created in their final form and remained unchanged. It presented a dynamic view of life, where species were constantly evolving and adapting to their environment.

The special creation of humans: Darwin's later work, "The Descent of Man," extended the theory of evolution to humans, suggesting that humans shared a common ancestor with apes. This challenged the anthropocentric view that humans were uniquely created in God's image and placed at the pinnacle of creation.

The role of a divine creator: While Darwin himself did not explicitly deny the existence of God, his theory offered a naturalistic explanation for the diversity of life, without the need for divine intervention. This challenged the traditional view of God as the creator and sustainer of all life.

The Impact on Agnosticism:

Darwin's theory of evolution had a significant impact on the development of agnosticism in several ways:

Providing a naturalistic explanation for the world: Evolutionary theory offered a compelling alternative to religious explanations for the origins and diversity of life. This undermined the authority of religious doctrines and encouraged a more naturalistic worldview, which resonated with agnostic perspectives.

Challenging the anthropocentric view of the universe: By placing humans within the broader context of evolutionary history, Darwin's theory challenged the anthropocentric view that humans were the center of creation. This encouraged a more humble and realistic view of humanity's place in the universe, which aligned with the agnostic emphasis on the limitations of human knowledge.

Promoting scientific inquiry and critical thinking: The controversy surrounding Darwin's theory highlighted the importance of scientific inquiry and critical thinking in the pursuit of knowledge. This fostered a climate of intellectual curiosity and openness to new ideas that supported the development of agnosticism.

Agnostic Responses to Evolution:

Agnostics generally embraced Darwin's theory of evolution, seeing it as a triumph of scientific inquiry and a powerful tool for understanding the natural world. They saw no inherent conflict between evolution and agnosticism, as both emphasized the importance of evidence and acknowledged the limitations of human knowledge.

T.H. Huxley: Huxley, a close friend and supporter of Darwin, saw evolutionary theory as a cornerstone of scientific understanding and a powerful challenge to religious dogma. He actively defended Darwin's ideas and promoted the teaching of evolution in schools.

Herbert Spencer: Spencer, a philosopher and sociologist, applied evolutionary principles to social and cultural development, coining the phrase "survival of the fittest." While not strictly an agnostic, he advocated for a naturalistic worldview and emphasized the importance of individual liberty and self-reliance.

Continuing Debates:

The relationship between evolution and religion continues to be a source of debate and controversy today. While many religious individuals have reconciled their beliefs with evolutionary theory, others continue to reject it, citing perceived conflicts with religious doctrines. However, for agnostics, evolution remains a compelling example of the power of scientific inquiry to illuminate the natural world and challenge traditional beliefs.

Darwin's theory of evolution had a profound impact on the development of agnosticism, providing a naturalistic explanation for the diversity of life, challenging anthropocentric views, and promoting scientific inquiry and critical thinking. Agnostics generally embraced evolutionary theory, seeing it as a powerful tool for understanding the natural world and a testament to the importance of evidence-based reasoning. The ongoing debates surrounding evolution highlight the enduring tension between science and religion and the continuing relevance of agnosticism as a way to navigate the complexities of knowledge and belief in a world shaped by scientific discovery.

Chapter 8
Agnosticism and Religion

Agnosticism and religion are often perceived as mutually exclusive. However, the relationship between the two is far more complex and nuanced than simple opposition. This chapter delves into the intricate relationship between agnosticism and religion, exploring the various ways in which agnostics engage with religious beliefs, practices, and institutions. We will examine the spectrum of views within agnosticism regarding religion, from those who see it as incompatible to those who find ways to reconcile the two.

Defining the Relationship:

It's crucial to remember that agnosticism primarily addresses the epistemological question of whether it's possible to know with certainty if God exists. It doesn't inherently dictate a specific attitude towards religion or religious practices. This means agnostics can hold a wide range of views on religion, from complete rejection to active participation in religious communities.

Agnosticism and Religious Belief:

Incompatibility: Some agnostics view religious belief as inherently incompatible with their epistemological stance. They argue that since the existence of God is unknowable, it's intellectually dishonest to hold any firm belief about it. This perspective often leads to a rejection of organized religion and its doctrines.

Openness to Possibility: Other agnostics maintain an open mind towards the possibility of God's existence, even though they acknowledge the lack of definitive proof. They may find value in religious teachings and practices, even without subscribing to their literal truth.

Spiritual Agnosticism: Some agnostics identify as "spiritual but not religious," seeking meaning and connection beyond the material world without adhering to specific religious doctrines. They may engage in practices like meditation, mindfulness, or exploring nature to cultivate a sense of spirituality.

Agnosticism and Religious Practice:

Non-participation: Agnostics who view religion as incompatible with their beliefs often choose not to participate in religious practices or belong to religious institutions. They may find alternative ways to find community and meaning, such as through secular humanist organizations or other community groups.

Selective Participation: Some agnostics may participate in certain religious practices or rituals that resonate with them, even if they don't fully subscribe to the underlying beliefs. This could include attending religious services for their cultural or social significance, or finding value in practices like meditation or prayer.

Cultural or Familial Participation: Many agnostics continue to participate in religious activities due to cultural or familial ties, even if they don't personally hold strong religious beliefs. This can be a way to maintain connections with loved ones and participate in cultural traditions.

Agnosticism and Religious Institutions:

Critical Engagement: Agnostics often engage critically with religious institutions, questioning their authority, dogma, and influence on society. They may advocate for secularism and the separation of church and state, ensuring that religious beliefs don't dictate public policy or infringe on individual rights.

Appreciation for Positive Contributions: While critical of certain aspects of religious institutions, many agnostics also recognize the positive contributions that religions have made to society. This could include promoting ethical values, providing social support networks, and inspiring art and culture.

Dialogue and Cooperation: Some agnostics actively engage in dialogue and cooperation with religious individuals and institutions, seeking common ground on issues of shared concern, such as social justice, environmental protection, or promoting peace and understanding.

Challenges and Opportunities:

The relationship between agnosticism and religion presents both challenges and opportunities:

Challenges: Agnostics may face social pressure to conform to religious norms or may be excluded from certain communities or events due to their lack of religious affiliation. They may also struggle with reconciling their agnostic views with the religious beliefs of loved ones.

Opportunities: Agnosticism offers a unique perspective that can bridge divides between religious and non-religious individuals. By emphasizing the importance of evidence, critical thinking, and open dialogue, agnostics can contribute to a more tolerant and understanding society.

The relationship between agnosticism and religion is complex and multifaceted. Agnostics hold a wide range of views on religion, from complete rejection to active participation in religious communities. While some agnostics see religion as incompatible with their epistemological stance, others find ways to reconcile the two, appreciating the cultural, social, and ethical dimensions of religion while maintaining their commitment to evidence-based reasoning and intellectual honesty. Ultimately, the relationship between agnosticism and religion is a personal one, shaped by individual experiences, values, and beliefs.

Chapter 9
Atheism and Agnosticism

Atheism and agnosticism are two distinct philosophical stances that often get conflated or misunderstood. Both involve a lack of belief in God, but they differ in their approach to knowledge and certainty. This chapter aims to clarify the distinctions between atheism and agnosticism, exploring their similarities, differences, and how they relate to each other in the broader spectrum of non-belief.

Defining Atheism:

Atheism is, in its simplest form, the absence of belief in the existence of God or gods. It's a positive assertion that denies the existence of any deity. Atheists may arrive at this position through various means, including:

Reason and Evidence: Many atheists base their disbelief on the lack of compelling evidence for the existence of God and the prevalence of natural explanations for phenomena previously attributed to divine intervention.

Logical Arguments: Some atheists employ philosophical arguments, such as the problem of evil or the incompatibility of divine attributes, to demonstrate the inconsistency or improbability of God's existence.

Scientific Understanding: The advancements in science, particularly in fields like cosmology and evolutionary biology, have led some to conclude that a supernatural creator is unnecessary to explain the universe and its workings.

Defining Agnosticism (revisited):

Agnosticism, as we've explored in previous chapters, focuses on the knowability of God's existence. It's the view that it's impossible to know with certainty whether or not God exists.

Agnostics may emphasize the limitations of human knowledge, the lack of conclusive evidence, or the inherent nature of the question itself as reasons for their position.

Similarities between Atheism and Agnosticism:

Lack of Belief in God: Both atheists and agnostics share a lack of belief in God. Neither subscribes to the tenets of any particular religion or accepts the existence of a deity.

Rejection of Religious Dogma: Both stances tend to reject religious dogma and the authority of religious institutions. They emphasize the importance of reason, evidence, and critical thinking in forming beliefs about the world.

Overlap in Individuals: Many individuals identify as both atheist and agnostic, expressing both a disbelief in God and an acknowledgment of the unknowability of the divine.

Differences between Atheism and Agnosticism:

Nature of the Claim: Atheism is a positive assertion that denies the existence of God. Agnosticism, on the other hand, is a statement about knowledge, asserting the impossibility of knowing with certainty whether God exists.

Focus: Atheism focuses on the belief or disbelief in God, while agnosticism focuses on the possibility of knowledge about God's existence.

Certainty: Atheists express a degree of certainty in their disbelief, while agnostics emphasize the lack of certainty and the limitations of human knowledge.

The Spectrum of Non-belief:

Atheism and agnosticism can be seen as points on a spectrum of non-belief.

Strong Atheism: On one end of the spectrum is strong atheism (or "gnostic atheism"), which asserts with certainty that there is no God.

Agnostic Atheism: Many individuals fall somewhere in the middle, identifying as agnostic atheists. They both disbelieve in God and acknowledge the unknowability of the divine.

Agnostic Theism: While less common, some individuals identify as agnostic theists. They believe in God but acknowledge the lack of definitive proof.

Strong Agnosticism: On the other end of the spectrum is strong agnosticism, which asserts that the question of God's existence is inherently unknowable.

The Importance of Clear Definitions:

Understanding the distinctions between atheism and agnosticism is crucial for clear communication and avoiding misunderstandings. It's important to recognize that these are distinct philosophical positions, even though they share some common ground.

Common Misconceptions:

Agnosticism as a "fence-sitting" position: Agnosticism is often mischaracterized as a "fence-sitting" position between belief and disbelief. However, it's a distinct epistemological stance that acknowledges the limits of knowledge.

Atheism as requiring absolute certainty: While some atheists express strong convictions, atheism doesn't necessarily require absolute certainty. It's primarily about the absence of belief, not the absolute denial of possibility.

Atheism and agnosticism are distinct but related philosophical stances that share a lack of belief in God. While atheism is a positive assertion that denies God's existence, agnosticism focuses on the knowability of the divine, acknowledging the limitations of human knowledge. Understanding the nuances of these two positions allows for clearer communication and a more nuanced understanding of the spectrum of non-belief.

Chapter 10
Deism and Agnosticism

Deism and agnosticism, while distinct philosophical positions, share some common ground in their approach to the divine and the limitations of human knowledge. Both stand apart from traditional theistic religions, offering alternative perspectives on the existence and nature of God. This chapter explores the relationship between deism and agnosticism, examining their similarities, differences, and how they navigate questions of faith, reason, and the role of a creator in the universe.

Defining Deism:

Deism is a philosophical belief that posits the existence of a creator God who designed the universe and set it in motion but does not intervene in its affairs or the lives of individuals. Deists typically reject revealed religion, miracles, and divine intervention, emphasizing reason and observation as the primary sources of knowledge about the natural world and the creator.

Key Characteristics of Deism:

Belief in a Creator God: Deists believe in a supreme being who created the universe and its natural laws. This creator is often seen as a rational and benevolent force, responsible for the order and design of the cosmos.

Rejection of Revealed Religion: Deists typically reject organized religion and its reliance on sacred texts, prophets, and divine revelation. They see these as human constructs that often obscure the true nature of the creator and the universe.

Emphasis on Reason and Natural Law: Deists emphasize the importance of reason and observation in understanding the world. They believe that the universe operates according to natural laws that can be discovered through scientific inquiry.

Rejection of Miracles and Divine Intervention: Deists reject the notion of miracles and divine intervention in the natural world. They see these as violations of the natural order and incompatible with a rational understanding of the universe.

Similarities between Deism and Agnosticism:

Emphasis on Reason and Evidence: Both deists and agnostics emphasize the importance of reason and evidence in forming beliefs about the world. They tend to be critical of religious dogma and the reliance on faith without evidence.

Rejection of Traditional Religious Authority: Both positions question the authority of traditional religious institutions and their interpretations of sacred texts. They advocate for individual autonomy in matters of faith and belief.

Acknowledging Limitations of Human Knowledge: Both deists and agnostics acknowledge the limitations of human knowledge, particularly when it comes to understanding the ultimate nature of reality and the divine.

Differences between Deism and Agnosticism:

Belief in a Creator: The most significant difference is that deists believe in the existence of a creator God, while agnostics remain uncertain about the existence of any deity. Deism is a form of theism, while agnosticism is a separate category that neither affirms nor denies the existence of God.

Nature of the Creator: Deists have a specific conception of God as a creator who does not intervene in the world, while agnostics, if they entertain the possibility of God, do not necessarily hold any specific beliefs about God's nature or actions.

Approach to Knowledge: While both value reason and evidence, deists tend to believe that reason can lead to knowledge about the creator and the universe, while agnostics emphasize the inherent limitations of human knowledge, particularly in the realm of the divine.

Deism and Agnosticism in Historical Context:

Both deism and agnosticism gained prominence during the Enlightenment era, when reason and scientific inquiry were challenging traditional religious authority. Deism appealed to those who sought a rational basis for belief in a creator, while agnosticism offered a more skeptical approach, acknowledging the limits of human knowledge.

Notable Deists and Agnostics:

Deists: Thomas Jefferson, Benjamin Franklin, and Voltaire were among the prominent figures who expressed deist views.

Agnostics: Thomas Henry Huxley, Charles Darwin, and Bertrand Russell are notable examples of thinkers who identified as agnostics.

Deism and agnosticism offer alternative perspectives on the existence and nature of God, both emphasizing reason and evidence while questioning traditional religious authority. Deists believe in a creator who does not intervene in the world, while agnostics remain uncertain about the existence of any deity. While distinct, both positions reflect a critical engagement with religious beliefs and a commitment to intellectual honesty in the pursuit of knowledge.

Chapter 11
Pantheism and Agnosticism

Pantheism, a philosophical perspective that equates God with the universe and all its contents, presents an intriguing contrast to agnosticism. While agnosticism emphasizes the unknowability of God, pantheism offers a definitive, albeit unconventional, answer to the question of God's nature and existence. This chapter explores the relationship between pantheism and agnosticism, examining their points of convergence and divergence, and how they navigate the complexities of belief, knowledge, and the nature of reality.

Defining Pantheism:

Pantheism, derived from the Greek words "pan" (all) and "theos" (god), asserts that God is everything and everything is God. The universe, in its entirety, is identified with the divine, encompassing all matter, energy, and consciousness. Pantheism rejects the notion of a personal God separate from the world, instead viewing the divine as immanent within the natural world.

Key Characteristics of Pantheism:

God is the Universe: Pantheism equates God with the totality of existence, encompassing all that is, was, and ever will be. The universe itself is considered divine, imbued with inherent sacredness.

Immanence of the Divine: God is not a separate entity residing outside the universe but is immanent within it, present in every aspect of reality. This implies a deep interconnectedness between all things and a sense of unity with the divine.

Rejection of a Personal God: Pantheism typically rejects the concept of a personal God who intervenes in the world, answers prayers, or judges human actions. The divine is seen as an impersonal force or principle that underlies all existence.

Reverence for Nature: Pantheists often have a deep reverence for nature, seeing it as a manifestation of the divine. They may find spiritual fulfillment in experiencing the natural world and connecting with its inherent beauty and complexity.

Similarities between Pantheism and Agnosticism:

Critical of Traditional Theism: Both pantheism and agnosticism challenge traditional theistic conceptions of God as a separate, personal being who intervenes in the world. They offer alternative perspectives that question anthropomorphic depictions of the divine.

Emphasis on the Natural World: Both perspectives place a strong emphasis on the natural world as a source of knowledge and meaning. While pantheists see the natural world as divine, agnostics often find meaning and wonder in its complexity and vastness.

Openness to Scientific Inquiry: Both pantheism and agnosticism are generally compatible with scientific inquiry and a naturalistic worldview. They see no inherent conflict between science and their respective perspectives on the divine.

Differences between Pantheism and Agnosticism:

Certainty about God's Existence: The most significant difference is that pantheism offers a definitive answer to the question of God's existence, identifying God with the universe. Agnosticism, on the other hand, emphasizes the unknowability of God's existence, suspending judgment on the matter.

Nature of God: Pantheism defines God as the totality of existence, an impersonal force or principle underlying all reality. Agnosticism, if it entertains the possibility of God, does not necessarily hold any specific beliefs about God's nature or attributes.

Approach to Knowledge: Pantheists often claim a direct experience or intuitive understanding of the divine through their connection with the natural world. Agnostics, while valuing experience, emphasize the limitations of human knowledge and the importance of evidence-based reasoning.

Pantheism and Agnosticism: Points of Convergence:

Despite their differences, pantheism and agnosticism can converge in certain ways:

Appreciation for the Mystery of Existence: Both perspectives acknowledge the vastness and mystery of the universe, recognizing that human understanding is limited.

Rejection of Dogmatism: Both challenge rigid religious doctrines and encourage open-mindedness and intellectual humility in the face of the unknown.

Ethical Implications: Both perspectives can inspire ethical behavior and a sense of responsibility towards the natural world and all living beings.

Challenges and Opportunities:

Challenges for Pantheists: Pantheism can be challenging to reconcile with traditional religious beliefs and practices. It may also face criticism from those who see it as a form of atheism or a denial of a personal God.

Challenges for Agnostics: Agnostics may find it difficult to fully embrace the definitive claims of pantheism, which may seem to contradict their emphasis on the unknowability of the divine.

Opportunities for Dialogue: Both perspectives can contribute to a richer understanding of the divine and the nature of reality. Engaging in dialogue can foster mutual respect and appreciation for diverse approaches to spirituality and belief.

Pantheism and agnosticism offer contrasting perspectives on the divine, with pantheism identifying God with the universe and agnosticism emphasizing the unknowability of God's existence. While distinct, both perspectives share a critical stance towards traditional theism, an appreciation for the natural world, and an openness to scientific inquiry. Exploring their points of convergence and divergence can deepen our understanding of the complex relationship between belief, knowledge, and the nature of reality.

Chapter 12
Gnosticism and Agnosticism

Gnosticism, an ancient religious and philosophical movement, stands in stark contrast to agnosticism. While agnosticism emphasizes the inherent limitations of human knowledge, particularly regarding the divine, Gnosticism claims access to special, revealed knowledge that unlocks the mysteries of the universe and humanity's place within it. This chapter explores the fascinating juxtaposition of Gnosticism and agnosticism, examining their core tenets, their historical context, and the fundamental differences that set them apart.

Defining Gnosticism:

Gnosticism, derived from the Greek word "gnosis" meaning "knowledge," encompasses a diverse collection of beliefs and practices that flourished in the first few centuries CE. Gnostics believed in a dualistic cosmology, where the material world is inherently flawed and a realm of spiritual enlightenment exists beyond it. They claimed access to secret knowledge, or "gnosis," which offered salvation and liberation from the material world.

Key Characteristics of Gnosticism:

Dualistic Cosmology: Gnostics viewed the universe as divided between the spiritual realm, which is perfect and divine, and the material realm, which is imperfect and corrupted. This material world is often seen as the creation of a lesser deity, the Demiurge, who is ignorant of the true, higher God.

Secret Knowledge (Gnosis): Gnostics believed that salvation could be achieved through the attainment of "gnosis," a special kind of knowledge revealed through divine intermediaries or inner enlightenment. This knowledge offered insights into the true nature of reality, the origin of the universe, and the human condition.

The Divine Spark: Gnostics believed that humans possess a divine spark, a fragment of the true God, trapped within their material bodies. Through gnosis, this divine spark could be awakened, leading to spiritual liberation and a return to the divine realm.

Rejection of the Material World: Gnostics often viewed the material world with disdain, seeing it as a source of suffering and illusion. They advocated for asceticism and detachment from material possessions and pleasures to pursue spiritual enlightenment.

Historical Context of Gnosticism:

Gnosticism emerged during a period of religious and intellectual ferment in the first few centuries CE, alongside early Christianity and other religious movements. It drew upon elements of various philosophical and religious traditions, including Platonism, Judaism, and Zoroastrianism. Gnostic texts, such as the Nag Hammadi library discovered in 1945, offer insights into their diverse beliefs and practices.

Similarities between Gnosticism and Agnosticism (however superficial):

Critical of Traditional Religion: Both Gnosticism and agnosticism, in their own ways, challenged the prevailing religious authorities of their time. Gnostics rejected the authority of orthodox religious institutions and their interpretations of scripture, while agnostics questioned the basis of religious beliefs and the possibility of knowing with certainty about the divine.

Emphasis on Individual Experience: Both perspectives, to some extent, emphasize the importance of individual experience in spiritual matters. Gnostics valued personal revelation and inner enlightenment, while agnostics prioritize individual autonomy in forming beliefs and seeking knowledge.

Fundamental Differences between Gnosticism and Agnosticism:

Approach to Knowledge: The most fundamental difference lies in their approach to knowledge. Gnostics claimed access to special, revealed knowledge that offered salvation and liberation. Agnostics, in contrast, emphasize the limitations of human knowledge, particularly regarding the divine, and advocate for intellectual humility and open-mindedness.

Certainty vs. Uncertainty: Gnosticism is characterized by a sense of certainty about the nature of reality and the path to salvation. Agnosticism, on the other hand, embraces uncertainty and acknowledges the possibility that some questions may remain forever unanswered.

The Nature of God: Gnostics believed in a complex cosmology with a hierarchy of divine beings, often including a supreme, unknowable God and a lesser creator deity. Agnosticism, if it entertains the possibility of God, does not necessarily hold any specific beliefs about God's nature or actions.

Attitude towards the Material World: Gnostics often viewed the material world with negativity, seeing it as a source of suffering and illusion. Agnostics, while acknowledging the challenges of the material world, do not necessarily reject it or advocate for complete detachment from it.

Gnosticism and agnosticism represent fundamentally different approaches to knowledge, belief, and the nature of reality. Gnosticism claims access to special, revealed knowledge that offers salvation and liberation, while agnosticism emphasizes the limitations of human knowledge and advocates for intellectual humility and open-mindedness. While both challenged the religious authorities of their time, their core tenets and methodologies stand in stark contrast. Understanding these differences highlights the diverse landscape of human thought and the various ways in which individuals have sought to make sense of the universe and their place within it.

Chapter 13
Epistemological Questions

Agnosticism, at its core, is deeply intertwined with epistemology, the branch of philosophy that explores the nature of knowledge, its limits, and how we acquire it. This chapter delves into the key epistemological questions that underpin agnostic thought, examining how agnostics approach knowledge claims, the role of evidence and reason, and the inherent limitations of human understanding.

What is Knowledge?

Epistemology grapples with fundamental questions about what constitutes knowledge. Is it simply true belief? Does it require justification or evidence? How can we distinguish between knowledge and mere opinion or belief? These questions are central to agnosticism, as it hinges on the idea that certain things, particularly those concerning the divine, may be beyond the realm of human knowledge.

Justified True Belief: A common definition of knowledge is "justified true belief." This means that to know something, it must be true, you must believe it, and you must have justification for your belief. Agnostics often apply this framework to religious claims, arguing that there is insufficient justification to warrant belief in the existence of God or other metaphysical entities.

Sources of Knowledge: Epistemology also explores the sources of knowledge. Are our senses reliable? Can we trust our reasoning abilities? What role does testimony from others play in acquiring knowledge? Agnostics often emphasize the importance of empirical evidence and rational inquiry as primary sources of knowledge.

Skepticism and the Limits of Knowledge: Skepticism, as discussed in Chapter 3, plays a crucial role in agnostic thought. Agnostics are often skeptical about the possibility of attaining absolute certainty, particularly when it comes to metaphysical claims. They acknowledge the potential for error, bias, and limitations in human understanding.

The Role of Evidence and Reason:

Agnosticism places a high value on evidence and reason in the pursuit of knowledge. Agnostics tend to be critical of claims that lack sufficient evidence or rely solely on faith or personal revelation. They emphasize the importance of:

Empirical Evidence: Evidence derived from observation and experience is crucial for agnostics. They often look to scientific inquiry and the natural world as sources of reliable knowledge.

Rational Inquiry: Agnostics value logical reasoning and critical thinking in evaluating knowledge claims. They are wary of fallacies, biases, and emotional appeals that can distort our understanding.

Fallibilism: Agnostics recognize that knowledge is always provisional and subject to revision in light of new evidence or arguments. They embrace the idea that our understanding of the world is constantly evolving.

Limitations of Human Understanding:

Agnosticism acknowledges the inherent limitations of human understanding. This recognition stems from various factors:

Cognitive Biases: Our minds are prone to various cognitive biases that can distort our perceptions and judgments. Agnostics are aware of these biases and strive to mitigate their influence on their thinking.

The Problem of Induction: The problem of induction highlights the limitations of drawing general conclusions from limited observations. Agnostics recognize that even with extensive evidence, we cannot be absolutely certain about the future or about universal claims.

The Nature of Reality: The nature of reality itself may pose limitations on our understanding. Some questions, particularly those concerning the ultimate nature of existence or the divine, may simply be beyond the grasp of human comprehension.

Agnosticism and Scientific Inquiry:

Agnosticism is often seen as compatible with scientific inquiry. Both emphasize the importance of evidence, reason, and critical thinking in the pursuit of knowledge. However, there are some key distinctions:

Scope: Science focuses primarily on the natural world and seeks to explain phenomena through natural laws and processes. Agnosticism, while supportive of science, also addresses broader questions about the nature of reality and the possibility of knowledge beyond the empirical realm.

Methodology: Science relies on empirical observation, experimentation, and hypothesis testing. Agnosticism, while valuing these methods, also recognizes the limitations of scientific inquiry and the potential for philosophical and introspective approaches to knowledge.

Agnosticism is deeply rooted in epistemological questions about the nature of knowledge, its limits, and how we acquire it. Agnostics emphasize the importance of evidence, reason, and critical thinking in evaluating knowledge claims, while acknowledging the inherent limitations of human understanding. They recognize that some questions, particularly those concerning the divine, may be beyond the reach of human knowledge. By grappling with these epistemological challenges, agnostics cultivate intellectual humility and open-mindedness in their pursuit of understanding the world and our place within it.

Chapter 14
Limits of Certainty

Agnosticism is fundamentally grounded in the recognition of the limits of certainty. It acknowledges that there are inherent boundaries to human knowledge and that absolute certainty, particularly regarding metaphysical claims, may be unattainable. This chapter explores the concept of the limits of certainty, examining the various factors that contribute to epistemic uncertainty, the implications for belief formation, and how agnosticism navigates the complexities of knowledge in the absence of absolute assurance.

The Quest for Certainty:
Throughout history, humans have sought certainty in various domains, from understanding the natural world to grasping the meaning of life and the existence of the divine. Certainty provides a sense of security, stability, and a foundation upon which to build beliefs and make decisions. However, the quest for absolute certainty often encounters obstacles and limitations.

Sources of Uncertainty:
Several factors contribute to the limits of certainty:

The Problem of Induction: As discussed in the previous chapter, the problem of induction highlights the limitations of drawing universal conclusions from limited observations. Even with extensive evidence, we cannot be absolutely certain that future observations will conform to past patterns.

Cognitive Biases: Our minds are susceptible to various cognitive biases that can distort our perceptions, interpretations, and judgments. These biases can lead to overconfidence in our beliefs and a tendency to overlook contradictory evidence.

The Underdetermination of Theory by Evidence: In many cases, multiple theories or explanations can account for the same set of evidence. This means that even with compelling evidence, we cannot be absolutely certain that we have arrived at the one true explanation.

The Nature of Reality: The nature of reality itself may pose limits on our ability to attain certainty. Some aspects of reality may be inherently complex, chaotic, or beyond the grasp of human comprehension.

Implications for Belief Formation:

The recognition of the limits of certainty has significant implications for how we form beliefs:

Fallibilism: Acknowledging the limits of certainty encourages a fallibilist approach to knowledge, recognizing that our beliefs are always provisional and subject to revision in light of new evidence or arguments.

Open-mindedness: Embracing uncertainty fosters open-mindedness and a willingness to consider alternative perspectives and interpretations. It discourages dogmatism and the clinging to beliefs in the face of contradictory evidence.

Intellectual Humility: Recognizing the limits of certainty cultivates intellectual humility, an awareness of the potential for error and a willingness to acknowledge the gaps in our understanding.

Agnosticism and the Limits of Certainty:

Agnosticism exemplifies the embrace of the limits of certainty. It acknowledges that the question of God's existence may be beyond the scope of human knowledge, and it avoids making definitive claims about the divine. Agnostics often emphasize:

The Importance of Evidence: While acknowledging the limits of certainty, agnostics still value evidence and reason in forming beliefs. They are willing to revise their views in light of new evidence or compelling arguments.

Suspension of Judgment: In the absence of conclusive evidence, agnostics often suspend judgment on metaphysical claims, recognizing that definitive answers may be unattainable.

The Value of Uncertainty: Agnostics do not necessarily see uncertainty as a negative state. They may view it as an opportunity for intellectual exploration, critical thinking, and a deeper appreciation for the mystery of existence.

Agnosticism and Practical Life:

Embracing the limits of certainty does not lead to paralysis or inaction. Agnostics can still make decisions and live meaningful lives even in the absence of absolute assurance. They may:

Base Decisions on Probabilities: While certainty may be elusive, we can often assess the probabilities of different outcomes and make decisions based on the available evidence and the potential consequences.

Develop Guiding Principles: Even without absolute certainty about the meaning of life or the existence of the afterlife, agnostics can develop ethical principles and values to guide their actions and choices.

Find Meaning in the Journey: Agnostics can find meaning and purpose in the pursuit of knowledge, the appreciation of beauty, the cultivation of relationships, and the contribution to something larger than themselves.

The recognition of the limits of certainty is a cornerstone of agnostic thought. It encourages a humble and open-minded approach to knowledge, recognizing the inherent boundaries of human understanding and the potential for error. While acknowledging the challenges of uncertainty, agnostics can still lead meaningful lives, guided by evidence, reason, and a commitment to intellectual integrity. By embracing the limits of certainty, agnostics cultivate a nuanced and sophisticated perspective on knowledge, belief, and the complexities of the human condition.

Chapter 15
Evidence and Belief

Agnosticism is intrinsically linked to the intricate relationship between evidence and belief. It emphasizes the importance of evidence in forming rational beliefs while acknowledging the limitations of evidence in proving or disproving certain claims, particularly those related to the divine. This chapter delves into the complex interplay between evidence and belief in the context of agnosticism, exploring the nature of evidence, the role it plays in shaping our beliefs, and how agnostics navigate the challenges of forming beliefs in the absence of conclusive evidence.

What is Evidence?

Evidence, broadly defined, is anything that provides support or justification for a belief or proposition. It can take various forms, including:

Empirical Evidence: This refers to evidence derived from observation, experience, and sensory perception. Scientific experiments, observations of natural phenomena, and personal experiences can all serve as empirical evidence.

Testimonial Evidence: This involves information or knowledge gained from the accounts or testimony of others. Expert opinions, historical records, and eyewitness accounts are examples of testimonial evidence.

Logical Evidence: This encompasses reasoning, arguments, and inferences that support a conclusion. Deductive reasoning, inductive reasoning, and abductive reasoning are all forms of logical evidence.

The Role of Evidence in Belief Formation:

Evidence plays a crucial role in shaping our beliefs about the world. It provides a foundation for rational belief formation, allowing us to assess the plausibility of different claims and make informed judgments.

Justification: Evidence serves as justification for our beliefs, providing reasons for why we hold certain views. The stronger the evidence, the more justified our beliefs become.

Revision of Beliefs: New evidence can challenge our existing beliefs and lead to their revision or rejection. A commitment to evidence-based reasoning requires a willingness to update our beliefs in light of new information.

Degrees of Belief: The strength of evidence often corresponds to the degree of confidence we have in our beliefs. Strong evidence leads to strong convictions, while weak or conflicting evidence may result in more tentative or uncertain beliefs.

Agnosticism and the Importance of Evidence:

Agnosticism emphasizes the importance of evidence in forming rational beliefs. Agnostics are often critical of beliefs that lack sufficient evidence or rely solely on faith, revelation, or dogma. They argue that:

Beliefs should be proportionate to the evidence: The strength of our beliefs should correspond to the strength of the available evidence. Extraordinary claims, such as the existence of God or miracles, require extraordinary evidence.

Evidence should be critically evaluated: Agnostics are mindful of the potential for biases, errors, and misinterpretations in evaluating evidence. They advocate for critical thinking and skepticism in assessing the reliability and validity of evidence.

The absence of evidence is not evidence of absence: Agnostics recognize that the lack of evidence for a claim does not necessarily prove its falsehood. However, it may warrant skepticism and a lower degree of belief.

Challenges of Evidence in Metaphysical Claims:

The relationship between evidence and belief becomes particularly complex when dealing with metaphysical claims, such as the existence of God, the afterlife, or the soul. These claims often lie beyond the realm of empirical investigation, making it challenging to gather definitive evidence.

The nature of metaphysical claims: Metaphysical claims often deal with concepts that are inherently abstract, intangible, and not directly observable. This makes it difficult to apply traditional scientific methods to gather evidence.

The limits of human understanding: As discussed in previous chapters, human understanding is inherently limited. Our cognitive biases, the problem of induction, and the nature of reality itself may pose challenges to attaining certainty about metaphysical claims.

Subjective experiences: While some individuals may cite personal experiences or religious revelations as evidence for metaphysical claims, these experiences are often subjective and difficult to verify objectively.

Agnosticism and the Absence of Conclusive Evidence:

In the absence of conclusive evidence for or against metaphysical claims, agnostics often adopt a position of:

Suspension of judgment: They may withhold belief in the existence of God or other metaphysical entities, recognizing that the evidence is insufficient to warrant a firm conviction.

Openness to possibility: While suspending judgment, agnostics may remain open to the possibility that future evidence or arguments could sway their perspective.

Focus on the knowable: Agnostics may choose to focus their attention on questions that are more amenable to empirical investigation and evidence-based reasoning, while acknowledging the limitations of human knowledge regarding metaphysical claims.

The relationship between evidence and belief is central to agnostic thought. Agnostics emphasize the importance of evidence in forming rational beliefs, while acknowledging the limitations of evidence in proving or disproving certain claims, particularly those related to the divine. They advocate for critical thinking, intellectual humility, and a willingness to revise beliefs in light of new evidence. In the absence of conclusive evidence, agnostics often suspend judgment on metaphysical claims, remaining open to the possibility of future discoveries while focusing their attention on questions that are more amenable to evidence-based inquiry.

Chapter 16
Burden of Proof

The concept of burden of proof is central to many debates and discussions, particularly those concerning the existence of God and other metaphysical claims. Agnosticism, with its emphasis on evidence and the limitations of knowledge, has a unique perspective on the burden of proof. This chapter explores the concept of burden of proof, its role in various contexts, and how it relates to agnostic thought.

What is Burden of Proof?

Burden of proof refers to the obligation to provide sufficient evidence or arguments to support a claim. In general, the person making a claim bears the burden of proving it. This principle is essential for rational discourse and helps to prevent unsubstantiated assertions from being accepted as true.

Burden of Proof in Different Contexts:

The burden of proof can vary depending on the context:

Legal Context: In legal proceedings, the burden of proof typically falls on the prosecution or plaintiff to prove their case beyond a reasonable doubt or by a preponderance of the evidence, respectively.

Scientific Context: In science, the burden of proof lies with the person proposing a new theory or hypothesis. They must provide sufficient evidence and arguments to convince the scientific community of its validity.

Everyday Discourse: In everyday conversations and debates, the burden of proof generally falls on the person making a claim, especially if it is a controversial or extraordinary claim.

Burden of Proof and the Existence of God:

The question of who bears the burden of proof in debates about the existence of God is a contentious one.

Theist Perspective: Theists often argue that the burden of proof lies with atheists to prove that God does not exist. They may claim that the existence of God is self-evident or that there is sufficient evidence in the natural world or religious experiences to support their belief.

Atheist Perspective: Atheists typically argue that the burden of proof lies with theists to prove that God does exist. They contend that extraordinary claims, such as the existence of a supernatural being, require extraordinary evidence.

Agnostic Perspective: Agnostics often take a more nuanced approach to the burden of proof. They may argue that:

The burden of proof lies with the person making a positive claim: Whether it is a theist claiming that God exists or an atheist claiming that God does not exist, the person making the positive assertion bears the burden of providing sufficient evidence.

The absence of evidence is not evidence of absence: Agnostics recognize that the lack of definitive proof for or against God's existence does not necessarily settle the matter. They may suspend judgment while remaining open to the possibility of future evidence or arguments.

The burden of proof can shift: In a debate, the burden of proof can shift back and forth as different arguments and evidence are presented. Agnostics may assess the strength of the arguments and evidence on both sides before forming a judgment.

Agnosticism and the Importance of Intellectual Honesty:

Agnostics often emphasize the importance of intellectual honesty in approaching the burden of proof. This involves:

Avoiding shifting the burden of proof inappropriately: It's important to avoid placing the burden of proof on the person who is questioning a claim rather than the person making the claim.

Being willing to acknowledge the limitations of one's own arguments and evidence: Agnostics recognize that their own arguments and evidence may not be conclusive and that there may be gaps in their understanding.

Being open to revising one's views in light of new evidence or arguments: Agnostics are committed to following the evidence where it leads, even if it challenges their existing beliefs.

Burden of Proof and Practical Implications:

The concept of burden of proof has practical implications for various aspects of life:

Decision-making: In making decisions, it's important to consider who bears the burden of proof for the different options. This can help to ensure that decisions are based on sound evidence and reasoning.

Critical thinking: Understanding the burden of proof can help to develop critical thinking skills and evaluate claims more effectively.

Ethical considerations: In ethical debates, the burden of proof often falls on the person advocating for a change in policy or behavior. This helps to ensure that changes are justified and based on sound moral reasoning.

The concept of burden of proof is crucial for rational discourse and informed decision-making. Agnostics, with their emphasis on evidence and the limitations of knowledge, take a nuanced approach to the burden of proof, recognizing that it can vary depending on the context and that the absence of conclusive evidence does not necessarily settle a matter. By upholding the principles of intellectual honesty and critical thinking, agnostics navigate the complexities of knowledge and belief while remaining open to revising their views in light of new evidence or arguments.

Chapter 17
Cosmological Arguments

Cosmological arguments are a family of philosophical arguments that attempt to prove the existence of God based on the existence of the universe or the cosmos. These arguments have a long history, dating back to ancient Greece, and continue to be debated by philosophers and theologians today. This chapter explores the various forms of cosmological arguments, their strengths and weaknesses, and how agnostics typically engage with these attempts to prove God's existence.

Types of Cosmological Arguments:

There are several variations of cosmological arguments, but they generally share a common structure:

1. **Premise:** Start with an observation about the universe, such as its existence, its beginning, or its order and design.
2. **Argument:** Argue that this observation requires an explanation, and that the best or only explanation is the existence of God.
3. **Conclusion:** Conclude that God exists.

Some common types of cosmological arguments include:

First Cause Argument (Kalam Cosmological Argument):

Premise: Everything that begins to exist has a cause. The universe began to exist.

Argument: Therefore, the universe has a cause. This cause must be uncaused and timeless, which is identified as God.

Argument from Contingency:

Premise: Everything in the universe is contingent, meaning it could have been different or not existed at all.

Argument: There must be a necessary being, one that exists by its own necessity and is not dependent on anything else, to explain the existence of contingent beings. This necessary being is identified as God.

- **Argument from Motion:**

Premise: Everything that is in motion is put in motion by something else.

Argument: There cannot be an infinite regress of movers. Therefore, there must be an unmoved mover, which is identified as God.

Strengths of Cosmological Arguments:

Intuitive Appeal: Cosmological arguments often have an intuitive appeal, as they resonate with the human desire to find explanations for the existence and nature of the universe.

Logical Structure: Many cosmological arguments have a logically valid structure, meaning that if the premises are true, the conclusion must also be true.

Focus on Fundamental Questions: These arguments address fundamental questions about the origin and nature of the universe, prompting deeper reflection on our place in the cosmos.

Weaknesses of Cosmological Arguments:

Questionable Premises: Critics often challenge the premises of cosmological arguments. For example, some argue that the universe may not have had a beginning, or that it is not necessarily contingent.

The Problem of Infinite Regress: Some argue that even if the premises are accepted, they do not necessarily lead to the conclusion that God exists. There may be alternative explanations, such as an infinite regress of causes or a multiverse.

The God of the Gaps: Cosmological arguments can be seen as "God of the gaps" arguments, where God is used to fill in the gaps in our scientific understanding. As science progresses and provides natural explanations for phenomena, the need for a divine explanation diminishes.

Agnostic Perspectives on Cosmological Arguments:

Agnostics typically engage with cosmological arguments with a critical but open mind. They may:

Acknowledge the strengths of the arguments: Agnostics may recognize the intuitive appeal and logical structure of cosmological arguments.

Scrutinize the premises and assumptions: They critically examine the premises and assumptions underlying the arguments, questioning their validity and considering alternative explanations.

Highlight the limitations of the arguments: Agnostics emphasize the limitations of these arguments in proving the existence of God with certainty. They may point out the possibility of alternative explanations or the lack of conclusive evidence.

Remain open to the possibility of God's existence: While acknowledging the limitations of cosmological arguments, agnostics may remain open to the possibility of God's existence, recognizing that these arguments may provide some support for theistic belief.

Cosmological arguments offer a line of reasoning for the existence of God based on observations about the universe. While these arguments have intuitive appeal and logical structure, they also face criticisms and limitations. Agnostics typically engage with cosmological arguments with a critical but open mind, acknowledging their strengths while scrutinizing their weaknesses. Ultimately, agnostics recognize that these arguments do not provide definitive proof for the existence of God, but they may contribute to the ongoing philosophical and theological discussions about the origin and nature of the universe and the possibility of a divine creator.

Chapter 18
Teleological Arguments

Teleological arguments, also known as arguments from design, offer another line of reasoning for the existence of God. These arguments focus on the apparent order, purpose, and complexity observed in the universe and argue that such features point to the existence of an intelligent designer, often identified as God. This chapter explores the various forms of teleological arguments, their historical development, their strengths and weaknesses, and how agnostics typically engage with these arguments.

What are Teleological Arguments?

Teleological arguments typically proceed as follows:

Premise: Begin with an observation about the apparent design or purpose in the universe, such as the intricate complexity of living organisms, the fine-tuning of physical constants, or the beauty and harmony of natural phenomena.

Argument: Argue that this apparent design is best explained by the existence of an intelligent designer, who intentionally created the universe with these features.

Conclusion: Conclude that an intelligent designer, often identified as God, exists.

Historical Development:

Teleological arguments have a long history, dating back to ancient philosophers like Plato and Aristotle.

Plato: In his work "Timaeus," Plato argued that the universe exhibits order and intelligence, suggesting the existence of a divine craftsman or Demiurge.

Aristotle: Aristotle's concept of "final causes" suggested that everything in nature has a purpose or goal, which implies the existence of a guiding intelligence.

William Paley: In the 18th century, William Paley presented a classic teleological argument in his book "Natural Theology." He used the analogy of a watchmaker to argue that the intricate design of a watch implies the existence of a watchmaker, and similarly, the complex design of the universe implies the existence of a divine designer.

Types of Teleological Arguments:

Argument from Analogy: This argument, like Paley's watchmaker analogy, draws an analogy between the design observed in the universe and the design of human artifacts, arguing that both require an intelligent designer.

Argument from Fine-Tuning: This argument focuses on the precise values of physical constants and the conditions necessary for life in the universe, arguing that this fine-tuning is best explained by the existence of a designer who intentionally set these parameters.

Argument from Irreducible Complexity: This argument, often used in the context of biological systems, claims that certain biological structures are so complex and interdependent that they could not have evolved gradually through natural selection, implying the need for an intelligent designer.

Strengths of Teleological Arguments:

Intuitive Appeal: Teleological arguments often have an intuitive appeal, as they resonate with the human tendency to see purpose and design in the world around us.

Explanatory Power: These arguments offer a potential explanation for the complexity, order, and apparent purpose observed in the universe.

Compatibility with Scientific Findings: Some teleological arguments, particularly those based on fine-tuning, draw upon scientific findings to support their claims.

Weaknesses of Teleological Arguments:

The Problem of Evil: The existence of suffering and evil in the world poses a challenge to teleological arguments, as it seems incompatible with the existence of an all-powerful and benevolent designer.

Alternative Explanations: Critics argue that there are alternative explanations for the apparent design in the universe, such as evolution by natural selection or the multiverse hypothesis.

Anthropomorphism: Some argue that teleological arguments rely on an anthropomorphic conception of God, projecting human qualities onto the divine.

Agnostic Perspectives on Teleological Arguments:

Agnostics typically engage with teleological arguments with a critical but open mind. They may:

Appreciate the beauty and complexity of the universe: Agnostics often share a sense of wonder and awe at the natural world and its intricate workings.

Acknowledge the strengths of the arguments: They may recognize the intuitive appeal and explanatory power of teleological arguments.

Scrutinize the premises and assumptions: They critically examine the premises and assumptions underlying the arguments, considering alternative explanations and the limitations of the arguments.

Remain open to the possibility of God's existence: While acknowledging the limitations of teleological arguments, agnostics may remain open to the possibility of God's existence, recognizing that these arguments may provide some support for theistic belief.

Teleological arguments offer a line of reasoning for the existence of God based on the apparent design and purpose observed in the universe. While these arguments have intuitive appeal and offer potential explanations for the complexity of the world, they also face criticisms and limitations. Agnostics typically engage with teleological arguments with a critical but open mind, appreciating their strengths while scrutinizing their weaknesses. Ultimately, agnostics recognize that these arguments do not provide definitive proof for the existence of God, but they contribute to the ongoing philosophical and theological discussions about the nature of the universe and the possibility of a divine creator.

Chapter 19
The Ontological Argument

The ontological argument stands apart from other arguments for the existence of God, such as cosmological and teleological arguments, which rely on observations about the universe. Instead, the ontological argument attempts to prove God's existence through reason alone, based on the very concept of God. This chapter delves into the intricacies of the ontological argument, its historical development, its various formulations, its strengths and weaknesses, and how agnostics typically engage with this unique attempt to demonstrate God's existence.

What is the Ontological Argument?

The ontological argument, in its essence, argues that the very concept of God, as the greatest conceivable being, necessarily entails God's existence. It suggests that God's existence is a logical necessity, not contingent on any empirical evidence or observation.

Historical Development:

The most famous formulation of the ontological argument was presented by Anselm of Canterbury in the 11th century.

Anselm's Argument: Anselm defined God as "that than which nothing greater can be conceived." He argued that even a fool who denies God's existence understands this concept. However, Anselm contended that it is greater to exist in reality than to exist only in the mind. Therefore, if God exists only in the mind, we can conceive of something greater, namely, a being that exists both in the mind and in reality. This contradicts the definition of God as the greatest conceivable being. Therefore, God must exist in reality.

Other Formulations:

Over the centuries, philosophers have presented various reformulations and variations of the ontological argument.

René Descartes: Descartes offered a version of the argument based on the idea that existence is a perfection. Since God is a perfect being, God must possess all perfections, including existence.

Gottfried Wilhelm Leibniz: Leibniz argued that the concept of God is possible, and if it is possible, it must exist, because a perfect being would necessarily exist.

Modal Ontological Argument: Contemporary philosophers have developed modal versions of the argument, which focus on the possibility and necessity of God's existence.

Strengths of the Ontological Argument:

A Priori Reasoning: The ontological argument relies on a priori reasoning, meaning it does not depend on empirical evidence or observation. It attempts to prove God's existence through reason and logic alone.

Conceptual Analysis: It engages in conceptual analysis, exploring the very definition of God and its implications.

Parsimony: It offers a seemingly simple and elegant argument for God's existence, without relying on complex observations or scientific findings.

Weaknesses of the Ontological Argument:

Questionable Premises: Critics challenge the premises of the ontological argument, such as the idea that existence is a perfection or that the concept of God necessarily entails God's existence.

The Problem of "Existence": Some argue that the ontological argument conflates the concept of existence with the property of existence. Just because we can conceive of a perfect being does not necessarily mean that such a being exists in reality.

Circular Reasoning: Critics may argue that the ontological argument is circular, assuming the conclusion (God's existence) in the premises.

Agnostic Perspectives on the Ontological Argument:

Agnostics typically engage with the ontological argument with a critical but inquisitive mind. They may:

Appreciate the ingenuity of the argument: Agnostics may recognize the intellectual effort and creativity involved in formulating the ontological argument.

Scrutinize the premises and assumptions: They critically examine the premises and assumptions underlying the argument, questioning their validity and considering alternative interpretations.

Highlight the limitations of the argument: Agnostics emphasize the limitations of the ontological argument in proving the existence of God with certainty. They may point out the possibility of logical fallacies or the lack of empirical support.

Remain open to the possibility of God's existence: While acknowledging the limitations of the ontological argument, agnostics may remain open to the possibility of God's existence, recognizing that this argument may contribute to the ongoing philosophical and theological discussions about the nature of the divine.

The ontological argument presents a unique attempt to prove God's existence through reason alone, based on the very concept of God. While this argument has intrigued philosophers for centuries and sparked ongoing debate, it also faces criticisms and limitations. Agnostics typically engage with the ontological argument with a critical but open mind, appreciating its ingenuity while scrutinizing its weaknesses. Ultimately, agnostics recognize that the ontological argument does not provide definitive proof for the existence of God, but it contributes to the rich tapestry of philosophical inquiry into the nature of the divine and the limits of human knowledge.

Chapter 20
The Problem of Evil

The problem of evil is a classic philosophical challenge to the existence of God, particularly a God who is believed to be all-powerful, all-knowing, and all-good. It poses the question of how the existence of evil and suffering in the world can be reconciled with the existence of such a God. This chapter explores the problem of evil in detail, examining its various formulations, proposed solutions, and how agnostics typically engage with this challenge to traditional theistic beliefs.

What is the Problem of Evil?

The problem of evil can be formulated in several ways:

Logical Problem of Evil: This version argues that the existence of evil is logically incompatible with the existence of an all-powerful, all-knowing, and all-good God. If God possesses these attributes, God would have the power and knowledge to prevent evil, and the goodness to want to do so. Therefore, the existence of evil implies that God does not possess all of these attributes.

Evidential Problem of Evil: This version acknowledges that the existence of evil may not be logically incompatible with God's existence, but argues that the amount and severity of evil in the world provide strong evidence against the existence of a God with traditional attributes.

Emotional Problem of Evil: This version focuses on the emotional and existential impact of suffering and evil, particularly when it seems gratuitous or senseless. It questions how a loving God could allow such suffering to occur.

Types of Evil:

Philosophers distinguish between different types of evil:

Moral Evil: This refers to evil caused by human actions, such as murder, theft, and cruelty.

Natural Evil: This refers to evil caused by natural events, such as earthquakes, floods, and diseases.

Proposed Solutions (Theodicies):

Theists have proposed various solutions, or theodicies, to the problem of evil:

Free Will Defense: This defense argues that God allows evil to exist because it is a necessary consequence of human free will. God could have created a world without evil, but it would be a world without free will, which is a greater good.

Soul-Making Theodicy: This theodicy suggests that evil and suffering are necessary for the development of human souls. Through facing challenges and overcoming adversity, humans develop virtues and grow spiritually.

Greater Good Theodicy: This defense argues that evil is permitted because it ultimately contributes to a greater good that we may not fully comprehend. God allows temporary suffering for the sake of a greater, ultimate good.

Challenges to Theodicies:

Theodicies face various challenges and criticisms:

The Severity of Evil: Some argue that the amount and severity of evil in the world, particularly gratuitous suffering, cannot be justified by any theodicy.

Natural Evil: Theodicies often struggle to account for natural evil, which is not directly caused by human actions.

The Hiddenness of God: If God allows suffering for a greater good, why is this greater good often hidden from us?

Agnostic Perspectives on the Problem of Evil:

Agnostics typically engage with the problem of evil with a sense of empathy and intellectual honesty. They may:

Acknowledge the profound impact of suffering: Agnostics recognize the reality of suffering and evil in the world and the challenges it poses to traditional theistic beliefs.

Critically evaluate theodicies: They examine the strengths and weaknesses of various theodicies, considering their explanatory power and their limitations.

Highlight the limitations of human understanding: Agnostics acknowledge that we may not fully comprehend the reasons for suffering or the nature of God's plan, if one exists.

Remain open to the possibility of God's existence: While acknowledging the challenge of the problem of evil, agnostics may remain open to the possibility of God's existence, recognizing that the problem of evil does not definitively disprove God's existence.

Focus on alleviating suffering: Agnostics may find motivation to address suffering and injustice in the world, even without relying on religious justifications.

The problem of evil is a profound philosophical challenge to the existence of an all-powerful, all-knowing, and all-good God. While theists have proposed various theodicies to address this problem, they face significant challenges and criticisms. Agnostics typically engage with the problem of evil with empathy and intellectual honesty, acknowledging its profound impact while remaining open to the possibility of God's existence. The problem of evil highlights the complexities of faith, the limits of human understanding, and the enduring quest to find meaning and purpose in a world filled with both beauty and suffering.

Chapter 21
Religious Experience

Religious experiences, often described as profound encounters with the divine or the transcendent, play a significant role in the lives of many people. These experiences can take various forms, from mystical visions and feelings of unity with the divine to moments of intense awe and wonder in the face of nature or religious rituals. This chapter explores the nature of religious experiences, their diverse forms, their psychological and neurological underpinnings, and how agnostics typically approach and interpret these experiences.

What are Religious Experiences?

Religious experiences are subjective experiences that are interpreted as encounters with the divine, the sacred, or the transcendent. They often involve a sense of connection to something larger than oneself, a feeling of awe and wonder, or a profound sense of meaning and purpose.

Types of Religious Experiences:

Mystical Experiences: These involve a sense of union or oneness with the divine or the ultimate reality. They often include feelings of transcendence, timelessness, and ineffability.

Numinous Experiences: These involve encounters with the sacred or the holy, often characterized by feelings of awe, reverence, and fear.

Conversion Experiences: These involve a sudden and dramatic change in one's religious beliefs or practices, often accompanied by a sense of being "born again" or transformed.

Prayer and Meditation: These practices can lead to experiences of deep connection with the divine, inner peace, and spiritual insight.

Nature Experiences: Encounters with the natural world, such as witnessing a breathtaking sunset or feeling the vastness of the ocean, can evoke a sense of awe and wonder that is interpreted as a religious experience.

Psychological and Neurological Perspectives:

Psychologists and neuroscientists have explored the psychological and neurological underpinnings of religious experiences.

Neurotheology: This field of study investigates the neural correlates of religious experiences, seeking to identify the brain regions and processes involved in these experiences.

Cognitive Science of Religion: This field explores how human cognitive processes, such as pattern recognition, agency detection, and theory of mind, contribute to the formation and interpretation of religious experiences.

Psychological Factors: Psychologists have identified various psychological factors that can contribute to religious experiences, such as personality traits, emotional states, and social influences.

Agnostic Perspectives on Religious Experiences:

Agnostics typically approach religious experiences with a combination of openness and critical inquiry. They may:

Acknowledge the power and significance of these experiences: Agnostics recognize that religious experiences can be deeply meaningful and transformative for individuals.

Seek natural explanations: They often explore natural explanations for religious experiences, considering psychological, sociological, and neurological factors that may contribute to these experiences.

Avoid drawing definitive conclusions about the divine: While acknowledging the subjective reality of religious experiences, agnostics avoid drawing definitive conclusions about the existence or nature of God based solely on these experiences.

Respect the diversity of interpretations: Agnostics recognize that religious experiences can be interpreted in various ways, depending on individual beliefs and cultural contexts.

Find value in spiritual practices: Some agnostics may engage in spiritual practices, such as meditation or mindfulness, even without subscribing to specific religious beliefs, to cultivate inner peace, self-awareness, and a sense of connection to something larger than themselves.

Challenges and Opportunities:

Challenges: Agnostics may face challenges in reconciling their skepticism about the supernatural with the deeply personal and often transformative nature of religious experiences.

Opportunities: Agnosticism offers a framework for engaging with religious experiences in a thoughtful and nuanced way, recognizing their significance while remaining open to natural explanations and avoiding dogmatic interpretations.

Religious experiences are complex and multifaceted phenomena that play a significant role in the lives of many people. Agnostics typically approach these experiences with a combination of openness and critical inquiry, acknowledging their power and significance while seeking natural explanations and avoiding definitive conclusions about the divine. By engaging with religious experiences in a thoughtful and nuanced way, agnostics can contribute to a deeper understanding of the human condition and the diverse ways in which people seek meaning and connection in the world.

Chapter 22
Faith and Reason

The relationship between faith and reason is a complex and enduring theme in philosophy and theology. It explores the interplay between belief, trust, and conviction on the one hand, and logic, evidence, and critical thinking on the other. This chapter delves into the intricate relationship between faith and reason, examining different perspectives on their compatibility, their potential conflicts, and how agnosticism navigates this dynamic interplay.

Defining Faith and Reason:

Faith: Faith can be understood as trust or confidence in something or someone, often in the absence of conclusive evidence or proof. It can involve belief in religious doctrines, trust in a higher power, or confidence in one's own intuition or values.

Reason: Reason encompasses the human capacity for logical thinking, critical analysis, and evidence-based inquiry. It involves the use of logic, observation, and inference to form judgments and draw conclusions.

Perspectives on Faith and Reason:

Throughout history, philosophers and theologians have offered various perspectives on the relationship between faith and reason:

Conflict: Some argue that faith and reason are inherently in conflict. They contend that faith relies on accepting beliefs without evidence or even in the face of contradictory evidence, while reason demands critical scrutiny and evidence-based justification.

Harmony: Others argue that faith and reason can coexist and even complement each other. They suggest that faith can provide a foundation for reason, while reason can help to clarify and refine religious beliefs.

Separation: Some propose that faith and reason operate in separate domains. They suggest that faith deals with matters of ultimate meaning and purpose, while reason deals with the empirical world and scientific inquiry.

Faith and Reason in Religious Contexts:

Different religious traditions have varying approaches to the relationship between faith and reason:

Fideism: This perspective prioritizes faith over reason, arguing that faith is the ultimate source of religious knowledge and that reason can be misleading or even detrimental to faith.

Rationalism: This perspective emphasizes the importance of reason in understanding religious truths. It suggests that reason can lead to knowledge of God and that religious beliefs should be consistent with rational principles.

Revelation: Many religious traditions rely on divine revelation as a source of knowledge. They believe that God has communicated truths to humanity through prophets, sacred texts, or religious experiences.

Agnosticism and the Interplay of Faith and Reason:

Agnostics typically approach the relationship between faith and reason with a nuanced perspective. They may:

Value both faith and reason: Agnostics recognize that both faith and reason play important roles in human life. Faith can provide comfort, hope, and a sense of purpose, while reason allows for critical thinking, problem-solving, and understanding the world.

Emphasize the importance of evidence: Agnostics prioritize evidence and reason in forming beliefs, particularly when it comes to claims about the existence and nature of God. They are critical of blind faith or accepting beliefs without sufficient justification.

Acknowledge the limits of reason: Agnostics also recognize the limitations of reason, acknowledging that there may be questions that lie beyond the reach of human understanding. They are open to the possibility that faith may provide insights or comfort in areas where reason falls short.

Advocate for intellectual humility: Agnostics encourage intellectual humility, recognizing the potential for error and bias in both faith-based and reason-based approaches to knowledge.

Promote dialogue and understanding: Agnostics often seek to bridge the gap between faith and reason, promoting dialogue and understanding between people with different perspectives.

Challenges and Opportunities:

Challenges: Agnostics may face challenges in navigating the tension between faith and reason, particularly when interacting with individuals who hold strong fideistic or rationalistic views.

Opportunities: Agnosticism offers a framework for engaging with both faith and reason in a thoughtful and balanced way, recognizing their respective strengths and limitations.

The relationship between faith and reason is a complex and multifaceted one, with various perspectives on their compatibility and interplay. Agnostics typically approach this relationship with nuance, valuing both faith and reason while emphasizing the importance of evidence, acknowledging the limits of reason, and promoting intellectual humility. By navigating the dynamic interplay between faith and reason, agnostics can contribute to a more thoughtful and understanding approach to knowledge, belief, and the search for meaning and purpose in life.

Chapter 23
Morality and Agnosticism

One common misconception about agnosticism is that it leads to moral relativism or nihilism. This chapter aims to dispel this myth by exploring the relationship between morality and agnosticism. We will discuss how agnostics can develop and maintain strong ethical frameworks without relying on religious beliefs or divine commands, drawing instead on reason, empathy, and human values.

Morality without God:
Many people associate morality with religion, believing that ethical principles are derived from divine commands or religious texts. However, agnostics demonstrate that morality can be grounded in secular and humanistic principles.

Reason and Logic: Moral philosophers have developed various ethical systems based on reason and logic, such as deontology (duty-based ethics) and consequentialism (consequence-based ethics). These systems provide frameworks for evaluating actions and making moral judgments based on rational principles.

Empathy and Compassion: Humans possess an innate capacity for empathy and compassion, which can serve as a foundation for moral behavior. Recognizing the shared humanity of others and understanding their perspectives can motivate us to act ethically and treat others with kindness and respect.

Human Values: Societies and cultures develop shared values, such as fairness, justice, and equality, that can guide moral decision-making. These values reflect our aspirations for a better world and can motivate us to work towards social progress and the well-being of all.

Sources of Agnostic Morality:

Agnostics can draw upon various sources to develop their moral compass:

Secular Humanism: Secular humanism emphasizes human reason, ethics, and justice, while specifically rejecting religious dogma, supernaturalism, pseudoscience, and superstition. It promotes a naturalistic worldview that focuses on human agency and responsibility in creating a more ethical and fulfilling life.

Universal Human Rights: The Universal Declaration of Human Rights, adopted by the United Nations in 1948, provides a comprehensive framework for human dignity and ethical behavior. It recognizes the inherent rights and freedoms of all individuals, regardless of their race, religion, or other characteristics.

Ethical Philosophies: Agnostics can draw inspiration and guidance from various ethical philosophies, such as Kantian ethics, utilitarianism, and virtue ethics. These philosophies offer different perspectives on moral decision-making and can help individuals to develop a well-reasoned and consistent ethical framework.

Personal Values and Experiences: Agnostics also develop their moral compass through personal reflection, life experiences, and interactions with others. They learn from their mistakes, cultivate empathy, and strive to live in accordance with their values.

Living an Ethical Life as an Agnostic:

Agnostics can lead ethical and fulfilling lives without relying on religious beliefs. They may:

Engage in critical reflection: Agnostics often engage in critical reflection about their values and beliefs, questioning assumptions and striving for intellectual honesty.

Cultivate empathy and compassion: They prioritize empathy and compassion in their interactions with others, seeking to understand different perspectives and promote the well-being of all.

Act with integrity and responsibility: They strive to act with integrity and take responsibility for their actions, recognizing their impact on others and the world around them.

Contribute to the greater good: Many agnostics find meaning and purpose in contributing to the greater good, working towards social justice, environmental sustainability, or other causes that align with their values.

Challenges and Opportunities:

Challenges: Agnostics may face challenges in defending their moral framework in a world where many people associate morality with religion. They may also encounter ethical dilemmas that require careful consideration and may not have easy answers.

Opportunities: Agnosticism offers a unique opportunity to develop a personalized and well-reasoned ethical framework based on human values, reason, and empathy. It encourages individuals to take ownership of their moral choices and contribute to a more ethical and just world.

Agnosticism does not lead to moral relativism or nihilism. Agnostics can develop and maintain strong ethical frameworks without relying on religious beliefs, drawing instead on reason, empathy, and human values. By engaging in critical reflection, cultivating compassion, and acting with integrity, agnostics can lead ethical and fulfilling lives, contributing to the greater good and promoting a more just and compassionate world.

Chapter 24
Secular Humanism

Secular humanism is a philosophical and ethical stance that emphasizes human reason, ethics, and justice while specifically rejecting religious dogma, supernaturalism, pseudoscience, and superstition. It is a worldview that places human beings at the center of moral concern, advocating for human agency and responsibility in creating a more ethical and fulfilling life. This chapter explores the principles of secular humanism, its historical development, its relationship to agnosticism, and its implications for individual and social life.

Key Principles of Secular Humanism:

Reason and Critical Thinking: Secular humanism emphasizes the importance of reason and critical thinking in understanding the world and making informed decisions. It encourages individuals to question assumptions, evaluate evidence, and form their own conclusions based on logic and evidence.

Ethics and Compassion: Secular humanism promotes a strong ethical framework based on human values, such as compassion, empathy, fairness, and justice. It encourages individuals to treat others with kindness and respect, and to work towards a more just and equitable society.

Human Flourishing: Secular humanism prioritizes human flourishing and well-being, both for individuals and for society as a whole. It encourages individuals to live meaningful and fulfilling lives, and to contribute to the betterment of humanity.

Naturalism: Secular humanism adopts a naturalistic worldview, seeing the universe as a natural phenomenon governed by natural laws. It rejects supernatural explanations and emphasizes the importance of scientific inquiry in understanding the world.

Human Agency and Responsibility: Secular humanism emphasizes human agency and responsibility in shaping our own lives and the world around us. It encourages individuals to take ownership of their choices and to work towards positive change.

Historical Development:

The roots of secular humanism can be traced back to ancient Greece and the Enlightenment, with its emphasis on reason and individual liberty. However, the modern secular humanist movement emerged in the 20th century, with the founding of organizations such as the American Humanist Association and the International Humanist and Ethical Union.

Relationship to Agnosticism:

Secular humanism and agnosticism share a close relationship. Both emphasize the importance of reason, evidence, and critical thinking, and both reject religious dogma and supernaturalism. Many agnostics identify as secular humanists, seeing it as a positive and ethical framework for living a meaningful life without relying on religious beliefs.

Implications for Individual and Social Life:

Secular humanism has implications for various aspects of individual and social life:

Ethics and Morality: Secular humanism provides a strong ethical framework based on human values and reason. It encourages individuals to make moral choices based on compassion, empathy, and a concern for the well-being of others.

Education: Secular humanism advocates for education that is based on reason, critical thinking, and scientific inquiry. It supports the separation of church and state and opposes religious indoctrination in public schools.

Social Justice: Secular humanism promotes social justice and equality, working towards a society where all individuals have the opportunity to flourish and reach their full potential.

Science and Technology: Secular humanism embraces science and technology as tools for understanding the world and improving human lives. It encourages responsible and ethical use of scientific advancements.

Meaning and Purpose: Secular humanism offers a framework for finding meaning and purpose in life without relying on religious beliefs. It encourages individuals to find fulfillment in their relationships, their work, their contributions to society, and their pursuit of knowledge and understanding.

Challenges and Opportunities:

Challenges: Secular humanism faces challenges in a world where religious beliefs are still prevalent and often hold significant influence. It may also be criticized for its perceived lack of spiritual dimension or its focus on human agency.

Opportunities: Secular humanism offers a positive and ethical framework for living a meaningful life in the 21st century. It provides a foundation for critical thinking, social progress, and human flourishing.

Secular humanism is a valuable worldview for agnostics and others who seek to live ethical and fulfilling lives without relying on religious beliefs. It emphasizes reason, compassion, and human agency, providing a framework for understanding the world, making moral choices, and contributing to the betterment of humanity. By embracing the principles of secular humanism, individuals can cultivate a rich and meaningful life based on human values, critical thinking, and a commitment to the greater good.

Chapter 25
Existentialism and Agnosticism

Existentialism, a philosophical movement that emphasizes individual freedom, responsibility, and the search for meaning in a seemingly meaningless universe, shares intriguing connections with agnosticism. Both grapple with questions of existence, purpose, and the human condition in the absence of absolute certainty or divine guidance. This chapter explores the relationship between existentialism and agnosticism, examining their shared concerns, their points of convergence and divergence, and how they navigate the challenges of finding meaning and purpose in a world without inherent meaning.

What is Existentialism?

Existentialism is a philosophical movement that emerged in the 19th and 20th centuries, emphasizing the following key ideas:

Existence Precedes Essence: Existentialists reject the notion that humans have a predetermined essence or purpose. Instead, they argue that our existence precedes our essence, meaning that we are born into a world without inherent meaning and are free to create our own essence through our choices and actions.

Freedom and Responsibility: Existentialism emphasizes the freedom and responsibility that comes with this lack of predetermined essence. We are free to choose who we want to be and what we want to value, but we are also responsible for the consequences of our choices.

Angst and Authenticity: The realization of our freedom and responsibility can lead to feelings of angst, anxiety, and despair. Existentialists encourage us to confront these feelings authentically and to create meaning in our lives despite the inherent absurdity of existence.

Subjectivity and Individuality: Existentialism emphasizes the importance of subjective experience and individual perspective. Each person's experience of the world is unique, and there is no objective truth or meaning that applies to everyone.

Shared Concerns of Existentialism and Agnosticism:

Existentialism and agnosticism share several common concerns:

The Absence of Certainty: Both acknowledge the limitations of human knowledge and the absence of absolute certainty, particularly regarding metaphysical questions.

The Search for Meaning: Both grapple with the challenge of finding meaning and purpose in a world without inherent meaning or divine guidance.

Individual Freedom and Responsibility: Both emphasize individual freedom and responsibility in shaping one's own life and values.

Rejection of Dogma: Both reject rigid doctrines and ideologies, encouraging individuals to think critically and form their own beliefs.

Points of Convergence:

Emphasis on Human Experience: Both existentialism and agnosticism prioritize human experience and subjective understanding in navigating the complexities of existence.

Authenticity and Self-Creation: Both encourage individuals to live authentically, creating their own values and meaning in life through their choices and actions.

Embrace of Uncertainty: Both acknowledge and even embrace the uncertainty and ambiguity of existence, seeing it as an opportunity for growth and self-discovery.

Points of Divergence:

Focus: Existentialism primarily focuses on the human condition, individual freedom, and the search for meaning.

Agnosticism focuses on the limitations of knowledge, particularly regarding the existence and nature of God.

Approach to the Absurd: Existentialists often emphasize the absurdity of existence, the lack of inherent meaning, and the need to create meaning in the face of this absurdity. Agnostics may acknowledge the absurdity of existence but may also find meaning and wonder in the natural world or human relationships.

Emotional Tone: Existentialism can be associated with a sense of angst, anxiety, and despair in the face of the human condition. Agnosticism tends to be more neutral in its emotional tone, emphasizing intellectual curiosity and open-mindedness.

Existentialism and Agnostic Thought:

Existentialism can complement and enrich agnostic thought by:

Providing a framework for meaning-making: Existentialism offers tools and perspectives for creating meaning and purpose in a world without inherent meaning or divine guidance.

Encouraging authentic living: It encourages agnostics to live authentically, making choices that align with their values and taking responsibility for their actions.

Promoting self-discovery: It invites agnostics to explore their own subjective experiences and create their own unique path in life.

Existentialism and agnosticism share a common ground in their acknowledgment of uncertainty, their emphasis on human experience, and their commitment to individual freedom and responsibility. While existentialism focuses on the human condition and the search for meaning, agnosticism focuses on the limitations of knowledge, particularly regarding the divine. By integrating existentialist insights, agnostics can develop a richer understanding of the human condition and find meaning and purpose in a world without inherent meaning or divine guidance.

Chapter 26
Free Will

The concept of free will, the ability to make choices and determine one's own actions, is a fundamental aspect of human experience. It underpins our notions of responsibility, morality, and meaning. However, the existence and nature of free will have been debated by philosophers and theologians for centuries. This chapter explores the concept of free will, its different interpretations, the challenges it faces from determinism and neuroscience, and how agnosticism approaches this complex and multifaceted issue.

What is Free Will?

Free will is generally understood as the capacity of agents to make choices that are up to them, that is, choices that are not entirely determined by external factors or prior events. It implies a degree of autonomy and self-determination in our actions and decisions.

Different Interpretations of Free Will:

Libertarian Free Will: This view holds that humans have genuine free will, meaning that our choices are not predetermined and that we have the power to choose otherwise in any given situation. This view is often associated with a non-materialist view of the mind or soul.

Compatibilist Free Will: This view argues that free will is compatible with determinism, the idea that all events, including human actions, are causally determined by prior events. Compatibilists argue that free will is not about having the ability to break the laws of causality, but rather about acting in accordance with one's desires and intentions, even if those desires and intentions are themselves determined.

Hard Determinism: This view denies the existence of free will altogether, arguing that all human actions are completely determined by prior events and that we have no genuine choice in the matter.

Challenges to Free Will:

Determinism: The philosophical idea of determinism poses a challenge to free will, as it suggests that all events, including human actions, are causally determined by prior events. If this is true, then it seems that our choices are not truly free, but rather predetermined.

Neuroscience: Recent findings in neuroscience have also raised questions about free will. Some studies suggest that brain activity associated with decision-making occurs before we are consciously aware of making a decision, implying that our conscious choices may be an illusion.

Agnostic Perspectives on Free Will:

Agnostics typically approach the question of free will with an open mind and a recognition of its complexities. They may:

Acknowledge the subjective experience of free will: Agnostics recognize that we have a strong subjective experience of making choices and determining our own actions.

Consider the philosophical arguments: They engage with the various philosophical arguments for and against free will, considering the strengths and weaknesses of different positions.

Remain open to the possibility of free will: Agnostics may remain open to the possibility of free will, even in the face of challenges from determinism and neuroscience, recognizing that the nature of consciousness and the mind-body problem are still not fully understood.

Emphasize responsibility and moral accountability: Regardless of the ultimate nature of free will, agnostics often emphasize the importance of taking responsibility for one's actions and holding oneself accountable for moral choices.

Focus on practical implications: Agnostics may focus on the practical implications of free will, such as the importance of promoting individual autonomy, encouraging ethical behavior, and fostering a sense of agency and purpose in life.

The question of free will is a complex and multifaceted one, with no easy answers. Agnostics typically approach this question with an open mind, acknowledging the subjective experience of free will, engaging with the philosophical arguments, and remaining open to the possibility of free will. Regardless of the ultimate nature of free will, agnostics often emphasize the importance of taking responsibility for one's actions and living an ethical and meaningful life.

Chapter 27
Consciousness and the Soul

The nature of consciousness and the existence of the soul are among the most profound and enduring mysteries that humans have pondered. Consciousness, our subjective awareness of ourselves and the world around us, seems to defy simple explanations. The soul, often conceived as the non-physical essence of a person, has been a central concept in many religious and philosophical traditions. This chapter explores the concepts of consciousness and the soul, examining different perspectives on their nature, their relationship to the brain and body, and how agnosticism approaches these enigmatic aspects of human existence.

What is Consciousness?

Consciousness is our subjective awareness of ourselves and our surroundings. It encompasses our thoughts, feelings, perceptions, and sense of self. Despite its central role in human experience, consciousness remains one of the most challenging phenomena to explain scientifically and philosophically.

Perspectives on Consciousness:

Materialism: Materialists argue that consciousness is a product of the physical brain and its processes. They believe that as neuroscience advances, we will eventually be able to explain consciousness entirely in terms of brain activity.

Dualism: Dualists propose that consciousness is separate from the physical body and brain. They believe in a mind or soul that exists independently of the material world.

Idealism: Idealists contend that consciousness is the fundamental reality and that the physical world is a manifestation of consciousness.

Integrated Information Theory: This theory proposes that consciousness arises from the complexity and integration of information within a system, such as the brain.

What is the Soul?

The soul is often conceived as the non-physical essence of a person, the seat of consciousness, identity, and personality. It is often associated with the idea of an afterlife and the possibility of continued existence after physical death.

Perspectives on the Soul:

Religious Perspectives: Many religions believe in the existence of a soul that is immortal and survives the death of the body. The soul is often seen as the divine spark within us or the part of us that connects to a higher power.

Philosophical Perspectives: Philosophers have debated the existence and nature of the soul for centuries. Some, like Plato, believed in an immortal soul that pre-exists the body and continues after death. Others, like Aristotle, saw the soul as the form or essence of a living being, inseparable from the body.

Scientific Perspectives: Science does not currently recognize the existence of a soul as a separate entity from the brain and body. However, some scientists and philosophers are exploring the possibility that consciousness may have non-local or quantum properties that could suggest a more complex relationship between mind and matter.

Agnostic Perspectives on Consciousness and the Soul:

Agnostics typically approach the questions of consciousness and the soul with an open mind and a recognition of their complexities. They may:

Acknowledge the mystery of consciousness: Agnostics recognize that consciousness is a profound mystery that continues to challenge scientific and philosophical understanding.

Consider different perspectives: They engage with various perspectives on consciousness and the soul, exploring the strengths and weaknesses of different viewpoints.

Remain open to the possibility of a soul: Agnostics may remain open to the possibility of a soul or some form of consciousness that transcends the physical body, while acknowledging the lack of definitive evidence.

Focus on the knowable: They may focus on the aspects of consciousness and the self that are more amenable to scientific inquiry and empirical investigation, such as the brain processes involved in perception, thought, and emotion.

Value the human experience: Agnostics appreciate the richness and complexity of human experience, including our capacity for love, creativity, and moral reasoning, regardless of the ultimate nature of consciousness or the existence of a soul.

The nature of consciousness and the existence of the soul remain among the most profound and challenging questions facing humanity. Agnostics typically approach these questions with an open mind, acknowledging the mystery of consciousness, considering different perspectives, and remaining open to the possibility of a soul while focusing on the knowable aspects of human experience. As science and philosophy continue to explore these enigmatic aspects of human existence, agnostics embrace the ongoing quest for understanding, recognizing that the full nature of consciousness and the self may forever remain a source of wonder and exploration.

Chapter 28
Life After Death

The question of what happens after death is one of the most profound and enduring mysteries that humans have contemplated. Many religions and spiritual traditions offer answers, promising an afterlife in various forms, from heavenly rewards to reincarnation. However, for agnostics, the question of life after death remains open, subject to the limitations of human knowledge and the absence of definitive evidence. This chapter explores the various perspectives on life after death, the arguments for and against an afterlife, and how agnosticism navigates this ultimate unknown.

Perspectives on Life After Death:
- **Religious Beliefs:** Many religions offer detailed descriptions of the afterlife, often involving rewards for the righteous and punishments for the wicked. Some common beliefs include:

Heaven and Hell: Many Abrahamic religions believe in a heaven, a realm of eternal bliss for those who have lived a virtuous life, and a hell, a place of eternal suffering for the unrepentant.

Reincarnation: Hinduism, Buddhism, and other Eastern religions believe in reincarnation, the cycle of birth, death, and rebirth, where the soul is reborn into new bodies based on its karma, or actions in past lives.

Ancestral Spirits: Many indigenous cultures believe that the spirits of the deceased continue to exist and can interact with the living.

Secular Perspectives: Secular perspectives on life after death vary:

Annihilationism: This view holds that consciousness ceases to exist after death, and there is no afterlife.

Transhumanism: This movement explores the possibility of extending human life through technology, potentially achieving immortality through artificial intelligence or other means.

Existentialism: Existentialists focus on the meaning and purpose we create in this life, recognizing that death is inevitable and that the afterlife is unknown.

Arguments for and Against an Afterlife:

Arguments for an Afterlife:

Near-Death Experiences: Some people who have come close to death report having profound experiences, such as seeing a light or feeling a sense of peace, which they interpret as evidence of an afterlife.

Religious Texts and Traditions: Many religious texts and traditions offer accounts of the afterlife, providing comfort and hope to believers.

The Desire for Continued Existence: The human desire for continued existence and the fear of annihilation may motivate belief in an afterlife.

Arguments Against an Afterlife:

Lack of Empirical Evidence: There is no scientific evidence to support the existence of an afterlife.

The Mind-Body Problem: The dependence of consciousness on the physical brain suggests that consciousness ceases to exist when the brain dies.

Parsimony: The principle of parsimony suggests that the simplest explanation is often the best, and the simplest explanation for death is that it is the end of individual consciousness.

Agnostic Perspectives on Life After Death:

Agnostics typically approach the question of life after death with an open mind and a recognition of the limits of human knowledge. They may:

Acknowledge the mystery of death: Agnostics recognize that death is a profound mystery and that the question of what happens after death may be beyond human comprehension.

Respect diverse beliefs: They respect the diverse beliefs and traditions surrounding life after death, understanding that these beliefs provide comfort and meaning to many people.

Avoid making definitive claims: Agnostics avoid making definitive claims about the existence or nature of an afterlife, recognizing the lack of conclusive evidence.

Focus on living a meaningful life: They focus on living a meaningful life in the present, recognizing that this life is finite and precious.

Find comfort in uncertainty: Some agnostics find comfort in the uncertainty of the afterlife, seeing it as an invitation to embrace the mystery of existence and appreciate the beauty of the present moment.

The question of life after death is a profound and enduring one, with no easy answers. Agnostics typically approach this question with an open mind, acknowledging the mystery of death, respecting diverse beliefs, and avoiding definitive claims. They focus on living a meaningful life in the present, recognizing the value of this life and the importance of making the most of the time we have. While the afterlife remains an unknown, agnostics embrace the uncertainty, finding meaning and purpose in the journey of life itself.

Chapter 29
Science and Agnosticism

Science and agnosticism share a deep and fundamental connection. Both are grounded in a commitment to evidence-based reasoning, critical inquiry, and a recognition of the limitations of human knowledge. This chapter explores the relationship between science and agnosticism, examining how they complement and inform each other, their shared values, and how agnosticism views the role of science in understanding the universe and our place within it.

Shared Values:

Evidence-Based Reasoning: Both science and agnosticism emphasize the importance of evidence in forming beliefs and drawing conclusions. They value empirical observation, experimentation, and logical reasoning as tools for understanding the world.

Critical Inquiry: Both encourage critical thinking and skepticism, questioning assumptions, evaluating evidence, and remaining open to revising beliefs in light of new information.

Fallibilism: Both recognize that knowledge is provisional and subject to revision. Scientific theories are constantly being refined and updated as new evidence emerges, and agnostics acknowledge that our understanding of the universe and the divine may always be incomplete.

Objectivity: Both strive for objectivity, seeking to minimize bias and personal preferences in the pursuit of knowledge. Scientists use rigorous methods to ensure the objectivity of their findings, and agnostics aim to approach questions of belief with intellectual honesty and impartiality.

How Science Informs Agnosticism:

Science provides valuable insights that inform and shape agnostic thought:

Naturalistic Explanations: Science offers natural explanations for phenomena that were once attributed to supernatural causes. This has led to a decline in superstitious beliefs and a greater appreciation for the power of natural processes.

The Vastness of the Universe: Scientific discoveries in cosmology and astronomy have revealed the vastness and complexity of the universe, challenging anthropocentric views and highlighting the limitations of human knowledge.

Evolutionary Biology: Darwin's theory of evolution provides a naturalistic explanation for the diversity of life on Earth, challenging traditional creationist beliefs and offering a new perspective on human origins and our place in the natural world.

Neuroscience: Advances in neuroscience are shedding light on the workings of the brain and its relationship to consciousness, challenging traditional notions of the soul and raising new questions about the nature of the self.

How Agnosticism Supports Science:

Agnosticism provides a philosophical framework that supports and encourages scientific inquiry:

Open-Mindedness: Agnosticism fosters an open-minded approach to knowledge, encouraging exploration and investigation without being constrained by dogmatic beliefs.

Intellectual Humility: Agnosticism promotes intellectual humility, recognizing the limitations of human knowledge and encouraging a willingness to revise beliefs in light of new evidence.

Freedom of Inquiry: Agnosticism supports freedom of inquiry, advocating for the right of scientists to pursue knowledge without interference from religious or political authorities.

The Limits of Science:

While agnosticism values and supports science, it also recognizes the limits of scientific inquiry:

Metaphysical Questions: Science primarily focuses on the natural world and empirical investigation. It may not be able to provide definitive answers to metaphysical questions about the existence of God, the nature of consciousness, or the meaning of life.

Ethical Considerations: Science can provide information and insights, but it cannot dictate ethical values or moral choices. Agnosticism recognizes the importance of ethical reflection and human values in guiding our actions and decisions.

Science and agnosticism share a deep and symbiotic relationship, grounded in a commitment to evidence-based reasoning, critical inquiry, and a recognition of the limitations of human knowledge. Science provides valuable insights that inform and shape agnostic thought, while agnosticism offers a philosophical framework that supports and encourages scientific inquiry. By embracing both science and agnosticism, we can cultivate a nuanced and comprehensive understanding of the universe and our place within it, while remaining open to the mysteries that may forever lie beyond our grasp.

Chapter 30
Naturalism

Naturalism is a philosophical worldview that posits that the natural world is all that exists, and that all phenomena can be explained in terms of natural causes and laws. This perspective has significant implications for how we understand the universe, ourselves, and our place in the cosmos. This chapter explores the core tenets of naturalism, its relationship to science, its implications for various areas of inquiry, and how it aligns with agnostic thought.

Key Principles of Naturalism:

The Primacy of the Natural World: Naturalism asserts that the natural world, the realm of matter, energy, and physical laws, is the only reality. There is no supernatural realm, no divine beings, or forces beyond the natural world.

Explanatory Power of Science: Naturalism views science as the most reliable method for understanding the natural world. It emphasizes the explanatory power of scientific theories and the ability of science to provide natural explanations for phenomena.

Causality and Natural Laws: Naturalism posits that all events and phenomena are governed by natural laws and causal relationships. There are no miracles, supernatural interventions, or exceptions to the laws of nature.

Methodological Naturalism: This principle, often employed in science, restricts scientific inquiry to natural explanations, excluding supernatural or divine explanations from consideration.

Ontological Naturalism: This is a stronger form of naturalism that asserts that only natural entities and properties exist. It denies the existence of any supernatural or spiritual realities.

Relationship to Science:

Naturalism and science share a close relationship. Science provides evidence and support for naturalistic explanations of the world, while naturalism provides a philosophical framework that guides scientific inquiry.

Evidence from Science: Scientific discoveries in fields such as cosmology, evolutionary biology, and neuroscience provide strong support for a naturalistic worldview. These discoveries offer natural explanations for the origin of the universe, the diversity of life, and the workings of the human brain.

Methodological Naturalism in Science: Scientists often employ methodological naturalism in their research, seeking natural explanations for phenomena and excluding supernatural explanations from consideration. This approach has been highly successful in advancing scientific knowledge.

Implications of Naturalism:

Naturalism has implications for various areas of inquiry:

Metaphysics: Naturalism rejects metaphysical claims that posit the existence of supernatural entities or realms. It offers a materialistic or physicalist view of reality, where everything can be explained in terms of matter and energy.

Epistemology: Naturalism views science as the most reliable source of knowledge about the natural world. It emphasizes empirical evidence, logical reasoning, and critical inquiry as the primary tools for acquiring knowledge.

Ethics: Naturalism grounds morality in natural human values, such as empathy, cooperation, and well-being. It rejects the idea that morality is derived from divine commands or religious texts.

Mind and Consciousness: Naturalism views consciousness as a product of the physical brain and its processes. It rejects the notion of a soul or a separate non-physical mind.

Naturalism and Agnosticism:

Naturalism aligns closely with agnostic thought. Both perspectives share a commitment to evidence-based reasoning, critical inquiry, and a recognition of the limitations of human knowledge. Many agnostics embrace naturalism as a worldview that is consistent with their skepticism about supernatural claims and their appreciation for the explanatory power of science.

Challenges and Criticisms:

Naturalism faces challenges and criticisms from various perspectives:

The Hard Problem of Consciousness: Some argue that naturalism struggles to account for the subjective experience of consciousness, the "what it's like" to be conscious.

The Problem of Moral Grounding: Critics question whether naturalism can provide a solid foundation for objective moral values and duties.

The Meaning of Life: Some argue that naturalism leads to nihilism or a sense of meaninglessness, as it rejects the existence of any higher purpose or divine plan.

Naturalism is a compelling worldview that offers a comprehensive and consistent understanding of the universe and our place within it. It aligns closely with agnostic thought, emphasizing the importance of evidence, reason, and scientific inquiry. While naturalism faces challenges and criticisms, it continues to be a valuable perspective for those who seek to understand the world in terms of natural causes and laws. By embracing naturalism, agnostics can find a framework for understanding the universe, themselves, and their place in the cosmos, while remaining open to the ongoing quest for knowledge and the mysteries that may forever lie beyond our grasp.

Chapter 31
Materialism

Materialism is a philosophical position that asserts that matter is the fundamental substance in nature, and that all things, including mental states and consciousness, are results of material interactions. It stands in contrast to dualism, which posits a separate realm of mind or spirit, and idealism, which holds that consciousness is the primary reality. This chapter explores the core tenets of materialism, its historical development, its implications for various areas of inquiry, and its relationship to agnosticism.

Key Principles of Materialism:

Matter is Fundamental: Materialism posits that matter is the fundamental constituent of reality. All things, including living organisms, minds, and consciousness, are ultimately composed of matter and its interactions.

Reductionism: Materialists often hold a reductionist view, believing that complex phenomena can be explained in terms of simpler, more fundamental physical processes. For example, they might argue that mental states can be reduced to brain states, or that biological processes can be reduced to chemical and physical interactions.

Causality and Physical Laws: Materialists believe that all events and phenomena are governed by physical laws and causal relationships. There are no supernatural interventions or exceptions to the laws of nature.

Mind-Body Identity: Materialism asserts that mental states are identical to brain states. This means that every mental state, such as a thought, feeling, or sensation, corresponds to a specific physical state in the brain.

Eliminative Materialism: This more radical version of materialism argues that our common-sense understanding of mental states is fundamentally flawed and that these concepts will eventually be eliminated as neuroscience progresses.

Historical Development:

Materialism has roots in ancient Greek philosophy, with thinkers such as Democritus and Epicurus proposing that the world is composed of atoms and void. However, materialism gained prominence in the modern era with the rise of science and the decline of religious authority.

Implications of Materialism:

Materialism has implications for various areas of inquiry:

Metaphysics: Materialism offers a monistic view of reality, where matter is the sole substance. It rejects dualism and idealism, denying the existence of any separate realm of mind or spirit.

Epistemology: Materialism views science as the most reliable method for understanding the natural world. It emphasizes empirical evidence, observation, and experimentation as the primary sources of knowledge.

Ethics: Materialism grounds morality in natural human values, such as well-being, flourishing, and social cooperation. It rejects the idea that morality is derived from divine commands or religious texts.

Mind and Consciousness: Materialism views consciousness as a product of the physical brain and its processes. It sees mental states as identical to brain states and denies the existence of a soul or a separate non-physical mind.

Free Will: Materialism often challenges traditional notions of free will, arguing that our actions may be determined by physical processes in the brain. However, some materialists argue that free will is compatible with determinism.

Materialism and Agnosticism:

Materialism aligns closely with agnostic thought. Both perspectives share a commitment to evidence-based reasoning, a naturalistic worldview, and a rejection of supernatural explanations. Many agnostics embrace materialism as a worldview that is consistent with their skepticism about the existence of a soul or an afterlife.

Challenges and Criticisms:

Materialism faces challenges and criticisms from various perspectives:

The Hard Problem of Consciousness: Some argue that materialism struggles to explain the subjective experience of consciousness, the "what it's like" to be conscious.

The Explanatory Gap: Critics point to an explanatory gap between physical processes in the brain and subjective mental states. It is unclear how physical matter can give rise to subjective experience.

Moral Grounding: Some question whether materialism can provide a solid foundation for objective moral values and duties.

Materialism is a compelling worldview that offers a comprehensive and consistent understanding of the universe and our place within it. It aligns closely with agnostic thought, emphasizing the importance of evidence, reason, and a naturalistic worldview. While materialism faces challenges and criticisms, it continues to be a valuable perspective for those who seek to understand the world in terms of matter and its interactions. By embracing materialism, agnostics can find a framework for understanding the universe, themselves, and their place in the cosmos, while remaining open to the ongoing quest for knowledge and the mysteries that may forever lie beyond our grasp.

Chapter 32
Reductionism

Reductionism is a philosophical approach that seeks to explain complex phenomena in terms of simpler, more fundamental components or processes. It is a powerful tool for understanding the world, allowing us to break down complex systems into their constituent parts and analyze their interactions. This chapter explores the concept of reductionism, its various forms, its applications in different fields of inquiry, its limitations, and how it relates to agnostic thought.

What is Reductionism?

Reductionism, in its essence, is the idea that the whole can be understood by understanding its parts. It involves explaining complex phenomena by reducing them to simpler, more fundamental entities or processes.

Types of Reductionism:

Ontological Reductionism: This form of reductionism claims that the entities and properties at one level of reality are identical to entities and properties at a lower level. For example, it might claim that mental states are identical to brain states, or that living organisms are ultimately nothing more than collections of atoms.

Methodological Reductionism: This approach advocates for explaining phenomena by breaking them down into their constituent parts and studying those parts in isolation. It is often used in scientific research, where complex systems are analyzed by studying their individual components.

Theoretical Reductionism: This form of reductionism seeks to unify different theories or explanations by showing how one theory can be derived from or reduced to another. For example, it might aim to reduce chemistry to physics or psychology to neuroscience.

Applications of Reductionism:

Reductionism has been applied in various fields of inquiry:

Physics: Physics has seen great success in reducing complex phenomena to fundamental forces and particles. For example, the behavior of gases can be explained in terms of the motion of individual molecules.

Chemistry: Chemistry can be seen as a reduction of complex substances to their constituent elements and the interactions between them.

Biology: Biology has made significant progress by reducing complex organisms to their constituent cells and molecules. The discovery of DNA and the genetic code is a prime example of reductionism in biology.

Neuroscience: Neuroscience seeks to understand the brain and its functions by studying its constituent neurons and their interactions.

Psychology: Some approaches in psychology attempt to reduce mental states and behaviors to underlying brain processes.

Strengths of Reductionism:

Explanatory Power: Reductionism can provide powerful explanations for complex phenomena by breaking them down into simpler components.

Scientific Progress: Reductionism has been instrumental in driving scientific progress, allowing scientists to analyze complex systems and make new discoveries.

Unification of Knowledge: Reductionism can help to unify different fields of knowledge by showing how they are interconnected and can be explained in terms of common underlying principles.

Limitations of Reductionism:

Oversimplification: Reductionism can sometimes lead to oversimplification, neglecting the emergent properties that arise from the interactions of components in complex systems.

Loss of Context: By focusing on isolated components, reductionism can sometimes lose sight of the broader context and the relationships between different levels of reality.

The Problem of Consciousness: Reductionism faces challenges in explaining subjective experience and consciousness, which seem to defy simple reduction to physical processes.

Reductionism and Agnosticism:

Agnosticism is compatible with a nuanced understanding of reductionism. Agnostics appreciate the explanatory power of reductionism and its role in scientific progress, but they also recognize its limitations. They are mindful of the potential for oversimplification and the need to consider emergent properties and the broader context when explaining complex phenomena.

Reductionism is a powerful tool for understanding the world, but it is not without its limitations. Agnostics appreciate the value of reductionism in scientific inquiry and its ability to provide explanations for complex phenomena. However, they also recognize the importance of considering emergent properties, the broader context, and the limits of reductionism when dealing with complex systems, especially those involving consciousness and the human mind. By embracing a nuanced understanding of reductionism, agnostics can navigate the complexities of knowledge and belief, appreciating the interconnectedness of different levels of reality while remaining open to the mysteries that may forever lie beyond our grasp.

Chapter 33
Emergentism

Emergentism offers a compelling alternative to reductionism, acknowledging the complexity and interconnectedness of the natural world. It proposes that new properties and phenomena can emerge from the interactions of simpler components, properties that cannot be fully explained by examining the individual parts in isolation. This chapter explores the concept of emergentism, its various forms, its applications in different fields, its implications for understanding consciousness and the mind, and how it relates to agnostic thought.

What is Emergentism?

Emergentism is a philosophical perspective that emphasizes the emergence of novel properties and phenomena from the interactions of simpler components. It argues that the whole is greater than the sum of its parts, and that emergent properties cannot be fully predicted or explained by analyzing the individual components in isolation.

Key Principles of Emergentism:

Novelty: Emergent properties are genuinely new and distinct from the properties of the individual components. They arise from the interactions and relationships between the parts, not from the parts themselves.

Irreducibility: Emergent properties cannot be reduced to or fully explained by the properties of the individual components. They represent a higher level of organization and complexity.

Downward Causation: Emergentists often argue for downward causation, the idea that higher-level emergent properties can influence or causally affect the lower-level components from which they emerged.

Supervenience: Emergent properties are said to supervene on the lower-level properties, meaning that any change in the emergent properties must be accompanied by a change in the underlying components.

Types of Emergentism:

Strong Emergentism: This form of emergentism argues that emergent properties are fundamentally different from and irreducible to the properties of the individual components. It often posits that emergent properties have their own causal powers and can influence the lower-level components.

Weak Emergentism: This version of emergentism acknowledges the emergence of novel properties but maintains that they are ultimately explainable in terms of the underlying components and their interactions, although such explanations may be complex and challenging.

Applications of Emergentism:

Emergentism has been applied in various fields:

Physics: The properties of liquids, such as viscosity and surface tension, are seen as emergent properties arising from the interactions of individual molecules.

Chemistry: The properties of complex molecules, such as proteins and DNA, are considered emergent, arising from the interactions of their constituent atoms and bonds.

Biology: The behavior of organisms, such as flocking in birds or schooling in fish, is seen as an emergent property arising from the interactions of individual organisms.

Neuroscience: Consciousness and other mental phenomena are often considered emergent properties of the brain, arising from the complex interactions of neurons and neural networks.

Social Sciences: Social structures and institutions, such as markets or governments, are seen as emergent properties arising from the interactions of individuals.

Emergentism and Consciousness:

Emergentism offers a promising framework for understanding consciousness. It suggests that consciousness may emerge from the complex interactions of neurons and neural networks in the brain, a phenomenon that cannot be fully explained by examining individual neurons in isolation.

Emergentism and Agnosticism:

Emergentism aligns well with agnostic thought. Both perspectives acknowledge the complexity and interconnectedness of the natural world and recognize the limitations of reductionist approaches. Agnostics appreciate the ability of emergentism to account for the emergence of novel properties and phenomena, including consciousness, without resorting to supernatural explanations.

Challenges and Criticisms:

Emergentism faces challenges and criticisms:

Explanatory Gap: Some argue that emergentism still leaves an explanatory gap between the lower-level components and the emergent properties. It is unclear how exactly new properties arise from the interactions of simpler components.

Causation: The concept of downward causation, where emergent properties influence lower-level components, is debated and challenged by some philosophers.

Emergentism offers a valuable perspective for understanding the complexity of the natural world and the emergence of novel properties and phenomena. It aligns well with agnostic thought, providing a framework for understanding consciousness and other complex systems without resorting to supernatural explanations. While emergentism faces challenges and criticisms, it continues to be a valuable tool for those who seek to appreciate the interconnectedness and emergent nature of reality.

Chapter 34
Chaos and Complexity

Chaos and complexity theory offer a fascinating lens through which to view the universe, challenging traditional notions of order and predictability. These theories explore the dynamics of complex systems, where seemingly random behavior can arise from deterministic laws, and where small changes in initial conditions can lead to vastly different outcomes. This chapter delves into the concepts of chaos and complexity, their implications for various fields, their philosophical significance, and how they resonate with agnostic thought.

What is Chaos Theory?
Chaos theory is a branch of mathematics and physics that studies the behavior of dynamic systems that are highly sensitive to initial conditions. This sensitivity, often referred to as the "butterfly effect," means that even tiny changes in the starting conditions of a system can lead to dramatically different outcomes over time.

Key Concepts in Chaos Theory:
Sensitivity to Initial Conditions: This is the hallmark of chaotic systems. Small initial differences can amplify over time, leading to unpredictable and seemingly random behavior.

Strange Attractors: These are complex geometrical patterns that characterize the long-term behavior of chaotic systems. They represent a kind of order within the apparent randomness.

Fractals: Fractals are complex geometric shapes that exhibit self-similarity at different scales. They are often used to model chaotic systems and natural phenomena.

What is Complexity Theory?

Complexity theory studies complex systems, which are characterized by a large number of interacting components and emergent properties that arise from these interactions. These systems often exhibit non-linear behavior, feedback loops, and adaptation.

Key Concepts in Complexity Theory:

Emergence: Complexity theory emphasizes the emergence of new properties and behaviors from the interactions of simpler components.

Self-Organization: Complex systems can self-organize, spontaneously forming patterns and structures without external control.

Feedback Loops: Feedback loops, where the output of a system influences its input, play a crucial role in the dynamics of complex systems.

Adaptation: Complex systems can adapt to changing environments, learning and evolving over time.

Applications of Chaos and Complexity Theory:

Chaos and complexity theory have been applied in various fields:

Weather Forecasting: Weather patterns are highly chaotic, making long-term prediction difficult.

Climate Modeling: Climate systems are complex, with many interacting factors that contribute to climate change.

Ecology: Ecosystems are complex networks of interacting organisms and their environment.

Economics: Financial markets exhibit chaotic behavior and complex dynamics.

Social Systems: Social systems, such as cities and societies, are complex systems with emergent properties and unpredictable behavior.

Philosophical Implications:

Chaos and complexity theory have significant philosophical implications:

Challenge to Determinism: While chaotic systems are deterministic, their sensitivity to initial conditions makes their long-term behavior unpredictable in practice. This challenges traditional notions of determinism and predictability.

The Role of Chance: Chaos and complexity theory highlight the role of chance and contingency in the evolution of complex systems.

Emergence and Reductionism: Complexity theory challenges reductionist approaches, emphasizing the importance of emergent properties and the limitations of explaining complex systems solely in terms of their parts.

Chaos, Complexity, and Agnosticism:

Chaos and complexity theory resonate with agnostic thought in several ways:

Embrace of Uncertainty: Agnosticism acknowledges the limitations of human knowledge and the inherent uncertainty of the universe. Chaos and complexity theory reinforce this perspective, highlighting the unpredictable nature of complex systems.

Appreciation for Complexity: Agnostics appreciate the complexity and interconnectedness of the natural world. Chaos and complexity theory provide tools for understanding and appreciating this complexity.

Openness to New Ideas: Agnosticism encourages open-mindedness and a willingness to consider new ideas and perspectives. Chaos and complexity theory challenge traditional ways of thinking and offer new insights into the dynamics of the universe.

Chaos and complexity theory offer a fascinating lens through which to view the universe, challenging traditional notions of order and predictability. They highlight the sensitivity to initial conditions, the emergence of new properties, and the role of chance in complex systems. These theories resonate with agnostic thought, reinforcing the embrace of uncertainty, the appreciation for complexity, and the openness to new ideas. By engaging with chaos and complexity theory, agnostics can gain a deeper appreciation for the dynamic and unpredictable nature of the universe and our place within it.

Chapter 35
The Universe in Evolution

The universe is not a static, unchanging entity but a dynamic, evolving system. From the Big Bang to the formation of stars and galaxies, from the emergence of life to the development of human consciousness, the universe has been undergoing a continuous process of transformation for billions of years. This chapter explores the concept of the universe in evolution, examining the scientific evidence for this dynamic view, its philosophical implications, and how it aligns with agnostic thought.

Evidence for an Evolving Universe:

The Big Bang: The prevailing cosmological model suggests that the universe began with the Big Bang, a state of extremely high density and temperature, approximately 13.8 billion years ago. Since then, the universe has been expanding and cooling, leading to the formation of stars, galaxies, and other structures.

Stellar Evolution: Stars are not static objects but undergo a life cycle of formation, evolution, and eventual death. They are born from collapsing clouds of gas and dust, shine for billions of years through nuclear fusion, and eventually die, sometimes in spectacular supernova explosions that seed the universe with heavier elements.

Galactic Evolution: Galaxies, vast collections of stars, gas, and dust, also evolve over time. They interact with each other, collide, and merge, shaping their structure and composition.

Planetary Formation: Planets form from the remnants of star formation, coalescing from dust and gas in protoplanetary disks. They undergo geological processes, such as volcanism and plate tectonics, that shape their surfaces and atmospheres.

Emergence of Life: Life on Earth emerged from non-living matter through a process called abiogenesis. Once life arose, it diversified and evolved through natural selection, leading to the incredible variety of organisms we see today.

Human Evolution: Humans are a product of this evolutionary process, sharing a common ancestor with other primates. Our brains and cognitive abilities evolved over millions of years, leading to the development of language, culture, and consciousness.

Philosophical Implications:

The concept of the universe in evolution has profound philosophical implications:

Change and Impermanence: It highlights the dynamic and ever-changing nature of reality, challenging the notion of a static and unchanging universe.

Interconnectedness: It emphasizes the interconnectedness of all things in the universe, from the smallest particles to the largest structures.

Emergence and Complexity: It supports the idea of emergence, where new properties and phenomena arise from the interactions of simpler components.

Contingency and Chance: It highlights the role of contingency and chance in the evolution of the universe, challenging the notion of a predetermined or teleological universe.

Agnosticism and the Evolving Universe:

The concept of the universe in evolution aligns well with agnostic thought:

Embrace of Uncertainty: Agnosticism acknowledges the limitations of human knowledge and the inherent uncertainty of the universe. The evolving universe reinforces this perspective, highlighting the dynamic and unpredictable nature of reality.

Appreciation for Complexity: Agnostics appreciate the complexity and interconnectedness of the natural world. The evolving universe provides a framework for understanding this complexity and the ongoing processes of change and emergence.

Openness to New Discoveries: Agnosticism encourages open-mindedness and a willingness to revise beliefs in light of new evidence. The evolving universe invites us to embrace new discoveries and expand our understanding of the cosmos.

Rejection of Dogma: Agnosticism rejects rigid doctrines and fixed beliefs. The evolving universe challenges the notion of a static and unchanging truth, encouraging us to remain open to new possibilities and interpretations.

The universe is not a static entity but a dynamic, evolving system, undergoing continuous transformation on all scales, from the subatomic to the cosmic. This perspective has profound implications for our understanding of reality, challenging traditional notions of order, predictability, and purpose. Agnosticism embraces the concept of the evolving universe, recognizing the limitations of human knowledge, appreciating the complexity of the natural world, and remaining open to new discoveries and perspectives. By understanding the universe as a dynamic and evolving system, agnostics can find a framework for appreciating the interconnectedness of all things, the role of chance and contingency, and the ongoing emergence of new properties and phenomena.

Chapter 36
Origin of Life

The origin of life is one of the most fundamental and captivating questions in science. How did life arise from non-living matter on the early Earth? While a definitive answer remains elusive, scientists have made significant progress in understanding the processes that may have led to the emergence of life. This chapter explores the current scientific understanding of the origin of life, the conditions on early Earth, the key steps involved in abiogenesis, and how this knowledge aligns with an agnostic perspective.

Conditions on Early Earth:
The early Earth, formed around 4.5 billion years ago, was a vastly different place than it is today. The atmosphere was largely devoid of oxygen, and the planet was bombarded by asteroids and comets. However, amidst this chaotic environment, the conditions were ripe for the emergence of life.

Liquid Water: Water is essential for life as we know it, serving as a solvent for chemical reactions and a medium for transporting nutrients and waste. The early Earth had abundant liquid water, thanks to its distance from the sun and volcanic activity that released water vapor into the atmosphere.

Organic Molecules: Organic molecules, the building blocks of life, were present on the early Earth. These molecules could have formed through various processes, such as reactions in the atmosphere, hydrothermal vents, or delivery by meteorites.

Energy Sources: Energy is required to drive the chemical reactions necessary for life. The early Earth had abundant energy sources, including sunlight, lightning, and geothermal heat.

Key Steps in Abiogenesis:

Abiogenesis, the process by which life arises from non-living matter, is thought to have involved several key steps:

Formation of Organic Molecules: Simple organic molecules, such as amino acids and nucleotides, formed from inorganic matter.

Self-Assembly: These organic molecules self-assembled into more complex structures, such as proteins and nucleic acids.

Enclosure: These complex molecules became enclosed within membranes, forming protocells, the precursors to cells.

Replication: Protocells developed the ability to replicate, passing on their genetic information to their offspring.

Evolution: Protocells began to evolve through natural selection, leading to the diversification of life and the emergence of more complex organisms.

Scientific Research on Abiogenesis:

Scientists are actively researching the origin of life, conducting experiments and developing theories to explain how abiogenesis may have occurred:

Miller-Urey Experiment: This classic experiment demonstrated that organic molecules could form from inorganic matter under conditions simulating the early Earth's atmosphere.

RNA World Hypothesis: This hypothesis proposes that RNA, not DNA, was the primary genetic material in early life. RNA has both genetic and catalytic properties, making it a plausible candidate for the first self-replicating molecule.

Hydrothermal Vents: Hydrothermal vents, underwater volcanic vents that release chemicals and heat, are considered potential sites for the origin of life.

Protocell Research: Scientists are developing artificial protocells to study the self-assembly and replication of early life forms.

Agnosticism and the Origin of Life:

The scientific understanding of the origin of life aligns well with an agnostic perspective:

Naturalistic Explanation: Science offers a naturalistic explanation for the origin of life, without resorting to supernatural or divine intervention. This aligns with the agnostic emphasis on evidence-based reasoning and the rejection of supernatural explanations.

Openness to New Discoveries: Agnosticism encourages open-mindedness and a willingness to revise beliefs in light of new evidence. The ongoing research on abiogenesis invites us to embrace new discoveries and expand our understanding of how life emerged.

Appreciation for Complexity: Agnostics appreciate the complexity and wonder of the natural world. The origin of life highlights the remarkable ability of matter to self-organize and give rise to life.

Embrace of Uncertainty: Agnosticism acknowledges the limitations of human knowledge and the inherent uncertainty of the universe. The origin of life remains a mystery, but science continues to shed light on the processes that may have led to this remarkable event.

The origin of life is a captivating question that continues to inspire scientific inquiry. While a definitive answer remains elusive, scientists have made significant progress in understanding the conditions on early Earth and the key steps involved in abiogenesis. This knowledge aligns well with an agnostic perspective, offering a naturalistic explanation, encouraging open-mindedness, and appreciating the complexity and wonder of the natural world. As science continues to explore the origin of life, agnostics embrace the ongoing quest for knowledge and the mysteries that may forever lie beyond our grasp.

Chapter 37
Human Evolution

Human evolution is a captivating journey spanning millions of years, a testament to the power of natural selection and the incredible adaptability of life. From our primate ancestors to the emergence of Homo sapiens, our species has undergone remarkable transformations, shaping our physical characteristics, cognitive abilities, and social behaviors. This chapter delves into the key milestones in human evolution, the evidence that supports our understanding of this process, and how this knowledge aligns with an agnostic perspective.

Evidence for Human Evolution:

The evidence for human evolution comes from various sources:

Fossil Record: The fossil record provides a wealth of information about our ancestors, revealing a gradual progression of changes in physical characteristics over millions of years. Fossil discoveries, such as Lucy (Australopithecus afarensis) and the Turkana Boy (Homo erectus), provide crucial evidence for the transitions between different hominin species.

Comparative Anatomy: Comparing the anatomy of humans with other primates reveals striking similarities, indicating a shared ancestry. For example, the skeletal structure, dentition, and musculature of humans and chimpanzees share many common features.

Molecular Biology: DNA analysis provides compelling evidence for human evolution. By comparing the DNA sequences of humans and other primates, scientists can trace evolutionary relationships and estimate the timing of divergence between different lineages.

Archaeological Evidence: Archaeological findings, such as tools, artifacts, and cave paintings, provide insights into the cultural and technological development of our ancestors.

Key Milestones in Human Evolution:

Bipedalism: One of the earliest defining characteristics of the human lineage was bipedalism, the ability to walk upright on two legs. This adaptation freed our hands for tool use and carrying objects, and it may have also contributed to the development of larger brains.

Tool Use: Early hominins began using tools millions of years ago. Tools allowed our ancestors to access new food sources, defend themselves, and manipulate their environment.

Brain Expansion: Over millions of years, the brain size of hominins increased dramatically. This expansion allowed for the development of more complex cognitive abilities, such as language, abstract thought, and social intelligence.

Language Development: The emergence of language was a crucial milestone in human evolution. Language allowed for complex communication, cooperation, and cultural transmission.

Migration and Dispersal: Homo sapiens originated in Africa and gradually migrated to other continents, adapting to diverse environments and developing unique cultures.

Implications of Human Evolution:

Understanding human evolution has profound implications:

Our Place in Nature: It places humans within the broader context of the natural world, highlighting our connection to other living organisms and our shared evolutionary history.

The Nature of the Self: It challenges traditional notions of human uniqueness and the separation of humans from the animal kingdom.

Moral and Ethical Considerations: It raises questions about the origins of morality, altruism, and social behavior.

Agnosticism and Human Evolution:

The scientific understanding of human evolution aligns well with an agnostic perspective:

Naturalistic Explanation: Science offers a naturalistic explanation for human origins and development, without resorting to supernatural or divine intervention. This aligns with the agnostic emphasis on evidence-based reasoning and the rejection of supernatural explanations.

Openness to New Discoveries: Agnosticism encourages open-mindedness and a willingness to revise beliefs in light of new evidence. The ongoing research on human evolution invites us to embrace new discoveries and refine our understanding of our origins.

Appreciation for Complexity: Agnostics appreciate the complexity and wonder of the natural world. Human evolution highlights the remarkable ability of life to adapt, evolve, and give rise to complex organisms like ourselves.

Embrace of Uncertainty: Agnosticism acknowledges the limitations of human knowledge and the inherent uncertainty of the universe. While we have learned a great deal about human evolution, many questions remain unanswered, and our understanding is constantly evolving.

Human evolution is a captivating journey that has shaped who we are today. The scientific evidence from fossils, comparative anatomy, molecular biology, and archaeology provides a compelling picture of our evolutionary history. This knowledge aligns well with an agnostic perspective, offering a naturalistic explanation, encouraging open-mindedness, and appreciating the complexity and wonder of the natural world. As science continues to explore human evolution, agnostics embrace the ongoing quest for knowledge and the mysteries that may forever lie beyond our grasp.

Chapter 38
Artificial Intelligence

Artificial intelligence (AI) is rapidly transforming the world around us, from self-driving cars and facial recognition software to medical diagnosis and personalized learning. AI raises profound questions about the nature of intelligence, consciousness, and the future of humanity. This chapter explores the concept of AI, its different types, its potential benefits and risks, and how it relates to agnostic thought.

What is Artificial Intelligence?

Artificial intelligence involves the development of computer systems that can perform tasks that typically require human intelligence, such as learning, problem-solving, decision-making, and language understanding. AI systems can be designed to mimic human cognitive abilities or to develop their own unique forms of intelligence.

Types of AI:

Narrow or Weak AI: This type of AI is designed to perform specific tasks, such as playing chess, translating languages, or recommending products. It excels in its designated domain but lacks general intelligence.

General or Strong AI: This hypothetical type of AI would possess human-level intelligence and be capable of performing any intellectual task that a human can.

Super AI: This hypothetical type of AI would surpass human intelligence in all aspects, potentially posing existential risks or opportunities for humanity.

Applications of AI:

AI has a wide range of applications across various fields:

Healthcare: AI is being used for medical diagnosis, drug discovery, personalized medicine, and robotic surgery.

Transportation: Self-driving cars and autonomous vehicles are being developed to improve safety and efficiency.

Finance: AI is used for fraud detection, risk assessment, and algorithmic trading.

Education: AI-powered personalized learning platforms can adapt to individual student needs and provide customized instruction.

Customer service: AI chatbots can interact with customers and provide support.

Benefits and Risks of AI:

AI has the potential to bring significant benefits to humanity:

Increased Efficiency and Productivity: AI can automate tasks, improve efficiency, and increase productivity in various industries.

Improved Healthcare: AI can help to diagnose diseases earlier, develop new treatments, and provide personalized care.

Enhanced Safety: AI-powered systems can help to prevent accidents and improve safety in transportation and other areas.

New Discoveries and Innovations: AI can assist in scientific research, leading to new discoveries and innovations.

However, AI also poses potential risks:

Job Displacement: AI-powered automation could lead to job displacement in certain industries.

Bias and Discrimination: AI systems can inherit biases from the data they are trained on, leading to discriminatory outcomes.

Privacy Concerns: AI systems can collect and analyze vast amounts of personal data, raising privacy concerns.

Existential Risks: The development of super AI could pose existential risks to humanity if not properly controlled.

AI and Agnosticism:

AI raises questions that resonate with agnostic thought:

The Nature of Intelligence: AI challenges our understanding of intelligence, raising questions about whether consciousness is necessary for intelligence and whether machines can truly think.

The Future of Humanity: AI raises questions about the future of humanity and our place in a world increasingly shaped by intelligent machines.

Ethical Considerations: AI development raises ethical concerns about bias, job displacement, and the potential for misuse. Agnostics emphasize the importance of ethical reflection and responsible innovation in the development and deployment of AI systems.

Artificial intelligence is a rapidly evolving field with the potential to transform our world in profound ways. It raises important questions about the nature of intelligence, the future of humanity, and the ethical implications of technology. Agnostics approach AI with a sense of curiosity and caution, recognizing both its potential benefits and risks. They emphasize the importance of evidence-based reasoning, critical thinking, and ethical reflection in navigating the challenges and opportunities presented by AI.

Chapter 39
The Future of Humanity

Humanity stands at a crossroads, facing unprecedented challenges and opportunities. Technological advancements, environmental changes, and social and political upheavals are shaping the trajectory of our species. This chapter explores the future of humanity from an agnostic perspective, considering the potential paths we might take, the challenges we face, and the values and principles that can guide us towards a more fulfilling and sustainable future.

Factors Shaping the Future:
Several key factors are shaping the future of humanity:

Technological Advancements: Rapid advancements in fields such as artificial intelligence, biotechnology, nanotechnology, and space exploration are transforming our world and creating new possibilities and challenges.

Environmental Changes: Climate change, resource depletion, and environmental degradation pose significant threats to human well-being and the planet's ecosystems.

Social and Political Trends: Globalization, demographic shifts, political polarization, and social inequalities are creating both opportunities and challenges for human societies.

Existential Risks: Humanity faces existential risks, such as nuclear war, pandemics, and catastrophic climate change, that could threaten the survival of our species.

Potential Futures:
The future of humanity is not predetermined. We have the power to shape our destiny through our choices and actions. Some potential futures include:

Technological Utopia: Technological advancements could lead to a future where poverty, disease, and suffering are eradicated, and humans enjoy extended lifespans and enhanced capabilities.

Sustainable Coexistence: Humanity could transition to a sustainable way of life, living in harmony with the planet's ecosystems and ensuring the well-being of future generations.

Dystopian Future: Environmental degradation, social unrest, or technological misuse could lead to a dystopian future characterized by conflict, inequality, and environmental collapse.

Extinction: Existential risks could lead to the extinction of humanity or a significant reduction in our population and capabilities.

Challenges and Opportunities:

Humanity faces several challenges in navigating the future:

Climate Change: Addressing climate change requires global cooperation, sustainable practices, and technological innovation.

Social Inequality: Reducing social inequality and ensuring equitable access to resources and opportunities is crucial for social stability and human flourishing.

Technological Risks: Managing the risks of artificial intelligence, biotechnology, and other emerging technologies requires careful ethical consideration and responsible innovation.

Existential Threats: Mitigating existential threats, such as nuclear war and pandemics, requires international cooperation and proactive measures.

However, humanity also has significant opportunities to create a better future:

Technological Solutions: Technological advancements can provide solutions to environmental challenges, improve healthcare, and enhance human capabilities.

Global Cooperation: International cooperation and collaboration are essential for addressing global challenges and ensuring a sustainable future.

Human Values: Human values, such as compassion, empathy, and justice, can guide us towards a more ethical and fulfilling future.

Agnosticism and the Future of Humanity:

An agnostic perspective offers valuable insights for navigating the future:

Embrace of Uncertainty: Agnosticism acknowledges the inherent uncertainty of the future and the limitations of human knowledge. This encourages a flexible and adaptable approach to planning for the future.

Critical Thinking: Agnosticism emphasizes critical thinking and evidence-based reasoning, which are essential for evaluating potential futures and making informed decisions.

Human Values: Agnosticism promotes human values, such as reason, compassion, and responsibility, as guiding principles for shaping a better future.

Hope and Action: While acknowledging the challenges, agnosticism encourages hope and action. It recognizes that humans have the agency to shape their future and that even small actions can make a difference.

The future of humanity is uncertain, but we have the power to shape our destiny through our choices and actions. Agnosticism offers a valuable perspective for navigating the future, emphasizing the importance of critical thinking, human values, and a willingness to embrace uncertainty. By facing the challenges and opportunities with courage, wisdom, and compassion, we can strive to create a future where humanity flourishes and thrives in harmony with the planet and each other.

Chapter 40
Agnosticism and Society

Agnosticism, while a personal philosophical stance, has profound implications for society. Its emphasis on reason, evidence, critical thinking, and ethical values can contribute to a more tolerant, just, and progressive society. This chapter explores the role of agnosticism in society, examining its impact on various social institutions, its contributions to public discourse, and the challenges and opportunities it faces in a world often shaped by religious and ideological beliefs.

Impact on Social Institutions:

Agnosticism can influence various social institutions:

Education: Agnosticism promotes a secular approach to education, emphasizing critical thinking, scientific inquiry, and the separation of church and state. It encourages open dialogue and the exploration of diverse perspectives, fostering intellectual curiosity and a respect for evidence-based reasoning.

Government and Law: Agnosticism advocates for secular governance, where laws and policies are based on reason, evidence, and human rights, rather than religious doctrines. It supports the separation of church and state, ensuring that religious beliefs do not dictate public policy or infringe on individual freedoms.

Healthcare: Agnosticism promotes a science-based approach to healthcare, emphasizing evidence-based medicine and patient autonomy. It supports access to comprehensive healthcare, including reproductive healthcare and end-of-life care, free from religious interference.

Media and Public Discourse: Agnosticism encourages responsible and ethical journalism, where information is presented objectively and critically. It promotes open dialogue and respectful debate on social and political issues, fostering a more informed and engaged citizenry.

Contributions to Public Discourse:

Agnosticism brings valuable perspectives to public discourse:

Critical Thinking and Skepticism: Agnosticism encourages critical thinking and skepticism, challenging dogma, questioning authority, and demanding evidence for claims. This contributes to a more reasoned and informed public discourse.

Tolerance and Respect for Diversity: Agnosticism promotes tolerance and respect for diverse beliefs and perspectives, recognizing that there is no one "right" answer to many questions. It encourages open dialogue and understanding between people with different worldviews.

Emphasis on Ethical Values: Agnosticism emphasizes ethical values, such as compassion, fairness, and justice, as guiding principles for social and political action. It promotes a humanistic approach to social issues, focusing on the well-being of all individuals.

Secularism and Freedom of Thought: Agnosticism advocates for secularism, ensuring that religious beliefs do not impose on public life or individual freedoms. It supports freedom of thought, expression, and conscience for all.

Challenges and Opportunities:

Agnosticism faces challenges in a world often shaped by religious and ideological beliefs:

Religious Influence: In many societies, religious institutions and beliefs hold significant influence over social and political life. Agnostics may face discrimination or social pressure to conform to religious norms.

Polarization and Intolerance: Increasing polarization and intolerance can make it challenging to engage in constructive dialogue and promote understanding between people with different worldviews.

Misconceptions and Stereotypes: Agnosticism is often misunderstood or misrepresented, leading to stereotypes and negative perceptions.

However, agnosticism also has opportunities to contribute to a more progressive society:

Growing Secularism: There is a growing trend towards secularism in many parts of the world, with increasing numbers of people identifying as non-religious. This creates opportunities for agnostics to engage in public discourse and promote secular values.

The Importance of Reason and Evidence: In an age of misinformation and disinformation, the agnostic emphasis on reason and evidence is more important than ever. Agnostics can play a vital role in promoting critical thinking and evidence-based decision-making.

Building Bridges: Agnosticism can serve as a bridge between religious and non-religious communities, fostering dialogue and understanding. By emphasizing shared values and common ground, agnostics can contribute to a more harmonious and inclusive society.

Agnosticism, with its emphasis on reason, evidence, critical thinking, and ethical values, has a vital role to play in shaping a more tolerant, just, and progressive society. It can influence social institutions, contribute to public discourse, and promote understanding between people with diverse worldviews. While agnosticism faces challenges in a world often shaped by religious and ideological beliefs, it also has opportunities to contribute to a more secular, reasoned, and compassionate society. By embracing agnostic values and engaging in constructive dialogue, we can work towards a future where all individuals are free to think for themselves, live ethically, and contribute to the greater good.

Chapter 41
Secularism

Secularism is a principle that advocates for the separation of religious institutions and beliefs from the affairs of government and public life. It promotes a neutral public sphere where individuals of all faiths and none are treated equally, and where public policy is based on reason, evidence, and human rights, rather than religious doctrines. This chapter explores the concept of secularism, its different forms, its historical development, its relationship to agnosticism, and its importance in promoting a tolerant and pluralistic society.

Key Principles of Secularism:

Separation of Church and State: Secularism seeks to separate religious institutions from government institutions, ensuring that religious beliefs do not dictate public policy or infringe on individual freedoms.

Freedom of Religion and Belief: Secularism guarantees freedom of religion and belief for all individuals, allowing them to practice their faith without interference from the state, while also protecting the rights of those who do not adhere to any religion.

Equality Before the Law: Secularism ensures that all individuals are treated equally before the law, regardless of their religious beliefs or lack thereof. It opposes any form of discrimination or privilege based on religion.

Neutrality of the Public Sphere: Secularism promotes a neutral public sphere where individuals of all faiths and none can participate freely without feeling pressured to conform to any particular religious viewpoint.

Reason and Evidence as Basis for Public Policy: Secularism advocates for public policy to be based on reason, evidence, and human rights, rather than religious doctrines. It encourages critical thinking and open dialogue on social and political issues.

Different Forms of Secularism:

State Secularism: This form of secularism emphasizes the strict separation of religious institutions from state institutions. It often involves a neutral stance towards religion, neither promoting nor inhibiting religious practice.

Laïcité: This French concept of secularism goes further than state secularism, actively promoting the absence of religious involvement in government affairs and public institutions. It often restricts religious expression in public spaces.

Positive Secularism: This approach recognizes the value of religious freedom and diversity while maintaining a neutral public sphere. It encourages interfaith dialogue and cooperation on issues of common concern.

Historical Development:

The roots of secularism can be traced back to ancient Greece and Rome, but it gained prominence during the Enlightenment, with thinkers like John Locke and Voltaire advocating for religious tolerance and the separation of church and state. The American and French Revolutions further solidified the concept of secularism in modern democracies.

Relationship to Agnosticism:

Secularism aligns closely with agnostic thought. Both emphasize the importance of reason, evidence, and critical thinking in forming beliefs and making decisions. Agnostics often support secularism as a way to ensure freedom of thought and conscience, protect individual rights, and promote a tolerant and pluralistic society.

Importance of Secularism:

Secularism plays a crucial role in promoting a tolerant and pluralistic society:

Protects Religious Freedom: By separating religion from government, secularism ensures that individuals are free to practice their faith without interference from the state.

Prevents Religious Discrimination: Secularism ensures that all individuals are treated equally before the law, regardless of their religious beliefs.

Promotes Social Harmony: Secularism fosters a neutral public sphere where individuals of all faiths and none can interact and participate without feeling pressured to conform to any particular religious viewpoint.

Encourages Reasoned Public Discourse: Secularism promotes public policy based on reason, evidence, and human rights, encouraging critical thinking and open dialogue on social and political issues.

Safeguards Individual Liberties: Secularism protects individual liberties, such as freedom of thought, expression, and conscience, from religious imposition.

Challenges and Criticisms:

Secularism faces challenges and criticisms:

Religious Opposition: Some religious groups oppose secularism, viewing it as a threat to their religious values and influence.

Cultural and Historical Context: The implementation of secularism can vary depending on cultural and historical contexts, leading to debates about the appropriate boundaries between religion and public life.

Balancing Religious Freedom with Other Rights: Balancing religious freedom with other fundamental rights, such as freedom of expression and equality, can be complex and require careful consideration.

Secularism is a vital principle for promoting a tolerant, just, and pluralistic society. It protects religious freedom, prevents religious discrimination, fosters social harmony, and encourages reasoned public discourse. While secularism faces challenges and criticisms, it remains a cornerstone of democratic societies and a valuable framework for ensuring that individuals of all faiths and none can live together in peace and mutual respect. Agnosticism, with its emphasis on reason, evidence, and individual autonomy, strongly supports secularism as a way to safeguard individual liberties and promote a society where all individuals are free to think for themselves and live according to their own conscience.

Chapter 42
Religious Tolerance

In an increasingly interconnected and diverse world, religious tolerance is essential for peaceful coexistence and social harmony. Religious tolerance means respecting and accepting the diverse religious beliefs and practices of others, even if they differ from one's own. It involves rejecting discrimination and prejudice based on religion and promoting understanding and dialogue between people of different faiths and none. This chapter explores the concept of religious tolerance, its importance, the challenges it faces, and how agnosticism contributes to a more tolerant and inclusive society.

What is Religious Tolerance?

Religious tolerance encompasses several key aspects:

Respect for Diverse Beliefs: It involves recognizing the right of individuals to hold their own religious beliefs, even if those beliefs differ from one's own.

Acceptance of Different Practices: It includes accepting the right of individuals to practice their religion freely, as long as those practices do not harm others or infringe on their rights.

Rejection of Discrimination: It means rejecting discrimination and prejudice based on religion, treating all individuals equally regardless of their faith.

Promotion of Understanding: It involves promoting understanding and dialogue between people of different faiths and none, fostering mutual respect and appreciation for diversity.

Freedom of Conscience: It includes respecting the right of individuals to change their religious beliefs or to have no religious beliefs at all.

Importance of Religious Tolerance:
Religious tolerance is crucial for several reasons:
Peaceful Coexistence: It allows people of different faiths and none to live together peacefully and respectfully, reducing the risk of conflict and violence based on religious differences.
Social Harmony: It fosters social harmony and cohesion by promoting understanding and acceptance between different religious communities.
Individual Freedoms: It protects individual freedoms, such as freedom of religion, belief, and conscience, allowing individuals to live according to their own values and convictions.
Enriched Society: It enriches society by promoting diversity and allowing for the exchange of ideas and perspectives between different religious and cultural groups.
Moral and Ethical Imperative: It is a moral and ethical imperative, recognizing the inherent dignity and worth of all individuals, regardless of their religious beliefs.
Challenges to Religious Tolerance:
Religious tolerance faces numerous challenges:
Religious Extremism: Religious extremism and intolerance can lead to violence, discrimination, and persecution of religious minorities.
Sectarianism and Prejudice: Sectarianism and prejudice within and between religious groups can create divisions and fuel conflict.
Misinformation and Stereotypes: Misinformation and stereotypes about different religions can lead to fear, mistrust, and discrimination.
Political and Social Tensions: Political and social tensions can exacerbate religious differences and lead to conflict.
Agnosticism and Religious Tolerance:
Agnosticism contributes to religious tolerance in several ways:
Emphasis on Reason and Evidence: Agnosticism encourages critical thinking and evidence-based reasoning, challenging dogma and promoting a more reasoned approach to

religious beliefs. This can help to reduce religious extremism and intolerance.

Respect for Diversity: Agnosticism promotes respect for diverse beliefs and perspectives, recognizing the limitations of human knowledge and the subjectivity of religious experiences. It encourages open dialogue and understanding between people of different faiths and none.

Secular Values: Agnosticism supports secular values, such as freedom of thought, expression, and conscience, which are essential for religious tolerance. It advocates for a neutral public sphere where individuals of all faiths and none are treated equally.

Ethical Framework: Agnosticism provides an ethical framework based on human values, such as compassion, empathy, and justice. This framework can guide individuals towards tolerant and respectful behavior towards others, regardless of their religious beliefs.

Religious tolerance is essential for peaceful coexistence, social harmony, and the protection of individual freedoms. It involves respecting diverse beliefs, accepting different practices, rejecting discrimination, and promoting understanding between people of different faiths and none. Agnosticism, with its emphasis on reason, evidence, respect for diversity, and secular values, plays a vital role in fostering religious tolerance and creating a more inclusive and harmonious society. By embracing agnostic values and engaging in constructive dialogue, we can work towards a world where individuals of all faiths and none can live together in peace and mutual respect.

Chapter 43
Freedom of Expression

Freedom of expression is a fundamental human right that allows individuals to express their thoughts, ideas, and beliefs without fear of censorship or reprisal. It is a cornerstone of democracy and a vital component of a free and open society. This chapter explores the concept of freedom of expression, its importance, its limitations, and its relationship to agnosticism.

What is Freedom of Expression?

Freedom of expression encompasses the right to:

Express Opinions: Individuals have the right to express their opinions on any matter, including political, social, religious, and artistic matters.

Seek and Receive Information: Individuals have the right to seek and receive information from various sources, including the media, the internet, and other individuals.

Impart Information: Individuals have the right to impart information and ideas to others, through speech, writing, art, or other forms of expression.

Freedom from Censorship: Individuals should be free from censorship by the government or other authorities, allowing them to express themselves without fear of reprisal.

Importance of Freedom of Expression:

Freedom of expression is crucial for several reasons:

Individual Autonomy: It allows individuals to express their individuality, develop their personality, and participate fully in society.

Truth-Seeking: It promotes the free exchange of ideas, allowing for the pursuit of truth and the challenging of falsehoods.

Democratic Governance: It enables citizens to hold their governments accountable, participate in public discourse, and make informed decisions.

Social Progress: It allows for the expression of dissent, the challenging of social norms, and the promotion of social change.

Creativity and Innovation: It fosters creativity and innovation in the arts, sciences, and other fields, allowing for the exploration of new ideas and perspectives.

Limitations on Freedom of Expression:

While freedom of expression is a fundamental right, it is not absolute. There are certain limitations that are generally accepted in democratic societies:

Incitement to Violence: Speech that directly incites violence or hatred against individuals or groups can be restricted.

Defamation: False statements that harm the reputation of another person can be subject to legal action.

Child Pornography: The production and distribution of child pornography is illegal and harmful.

National Security: In certain circumstances, restrictions on freedom of expression may be necessary to protect national security.

Agnosticism and Freedom of Expression:

Agnosticism strongly supports freedom of expression for several reasons:

Pursuit of Knowledge: Agnosticism emphasizes the importance of reason, evidence, and critical thinking in the pursuit of knowledge. Freedom of expression is essential for the free exchange of ideas and the challenging of beliefs.

Rejection of Dogma: Agnosticism rejects dogma and fixed beliefs, encouraging open-mindedness and the exploration of diverse perspectives. Freedom of expression allows for the questioning of authority and the challenging of established ideas.

Individual Autonomy: Agnosticism values individual autonomy and the right of individuals to form their own beliefs and express themselves freely. Freedom of expression is crucial for protecting this right.

Tolerance and Respect for Diversity: Agnosticism promotes tolerance and respect for diverse beliefs and perspectives. Freedom of expression allows for the peaceful coexistence of different viewpoints and fosters understanding between people with different worldviews.

Challenges to Freedom of Expression:

Freedom of expression faces numerous challenges in the modern world:

Censorship and Repression: Authoritarian governments and extremist groups often suppress freedom of expression to maintain control and silence dissent.

Hate Speech and Online Harassment: The internet and social media have amplified the spread of hate speech and online harassment, which can have a chilling effect on freedom of expression.

Misinformation and Disinformation: The spread of misinformation and disinformation can undermine public trust in information and make it difficult to engage in informed debate.

Freedom of expression is a cornerstone of democracy and a vital component of a free and open society. It allows for individual autonomy, the pursuit of knowledge, social progress, and creativity. Agnosticism strongly supports freedom of expression, recognizing its importance for critical thinking, the rejection of dogma, and the promotion of tolerance and diversity. While freedom of expression faces challenges in the modern world, it remains a fundamental right that must be protected and upheld. By embracing freedom of expression and engaging in responsible and respectful dialogue, we can foster a society where all individuals are free to express themselves and contribute to the vibrant exchange of ideas that drives human progress.

Chapter 44
Critical Thinking

Critical thinking is the ability to analyze information objectively, evaluate evidence, and form judgments based on reason and logic. It is an essential skill for navigating the complexities of the modern world, making informed decisions, and understanding the world around us. This chapter explores the concept of critical thinking, its key components, its importance in various contexts, and its relationship to agnosticism.

What is Critical Thinking?

Critical thinking involves:

Analyzing Information: Carefully examining information from various sources, identifying key ideas, and recognizing underlying assumptions and biases.

Evaluating Evidence: Assessing the quality and relevance of evidence, distinguishing between facts and opinions, and identifying logical fallacies and biases.

Forming Judgments: Drawing conclusions and making decisions based on reason, logic, and evidence, rather than emotion or intuition.

Problem-Solving: Applying critical thinking skills to solve problems, identify solutions, and evaluate outcomes.

Open-Mindedness: Being open to considering different perspectives and alternative viewpoints, even if they challenge one's own beliefs.

Self-Reflection: Reflecting on one's own thinking processes, identifying biases and assumptions, and striving for intellectual honesty.

Key Components of Critical Thinking:

Analysis: Breaking down information into its component parts, identifying key ideas, and recognizing relationships between different pieces of information.

Evaluation: Assessing the credibility and relevance of information, identifying biases and logical fallacies, and distinguishing between facts and opinions.

Inference: Drawing conclusions and making inferences based on available evidence and reasoning.

Interpretation: Understanding and interpreting information in context, considering different perspectives and possible meanings.

Explanation: Clearly and effectively communicating one's reasoning and conclusions to others.

Importance of Critical Thinking:

Critical thinking is crucial in various contexts:

Education: It helps students to learn effectively, evaluate information critically, and form their own judgments.

Workplace: It enables employees to solve problems, make informed decisions, and contribute to innovation.

Personal Life: It helps individuals to make informed choices about their health, finances, relationships, and other aspects of their lives.

Citizenship: It empowers citizens to participate in democratic processes, evaluate political candidates and policies, and engage in informed public discourse.

Science and Research: It is essential for conducting scientific research, evaluating evidence, and drawing valid conclusions.

Agnosticism and Critical Thinking:

Agnosticism strongly promotes critical thinking for several reasons:

Pursuit of Knowledge: Agnosticism emphasizes the importance of reason, evidence, and critical inquiry in the pursuit of knowledge. Critical thinking is essential for evaluating claims, assessing evidence, and forming rational beliefs.

Rejection of Dogma: Agnosticism rejects dogma and fixed beliefs, encouraging open-mindedness and the questioning of authority. Critical thinking allows for the challenging of established ideas and the exploration of alternative perspectives.

Skepticism and Doubt: Agnosticism embraces skepticism and doubt as tools for uncovering the truth. Critical thinking helps to identify biases, logical fallacies, and potential flaws in arguments.

Intellectual Humility: Agnosticism promotes intellectual humility, recognizing the limitations of human knowledge and the potential for error. Critical thinking encourages self-reflection and a willingness to revise beliefs in light of new evidence.

Developing Critical Thinking Skills:
Critical thinking skills can be developed through:

Education and Training: Formal education and training programs can provide individuals with the tools and techniques for critical thinking.

Practice and Application: Regularly engaging in critical thinking activities, such as analyzing arguments, evaluating evidence, and solving problems, can strengthen these skills.

Open Dialogue and Debate: Engaging in open dialogue and debate with others can expose individuals to different perspectives and challenge their own thinking.

Self-Reflection: Reflecting on one's own thinking processes, identifying biases and assumptions, and seeking feedback from others can improve critical thinking skills.

Critical thinking is an essential skill for navigating the complexities of the modern world and making informed decisions. It involves analyzing information objectively, evaluating evidence, and forming judgments based on reason and logic. Agnosticism strongly promotes critical thinking, recognizing its importance for the pursuit of knowledge, the rejection of dogma, and the development of intellectual humility. By embracing critical thinking and cultivating these skills, we can become more informed, engaged, and responsible individuals, contributing to a more reasoned and enlightened society.

Chapter 45
Scientific Skepticism

Scientific skepticism is a vital approach to evaluating claims and acquiring knowledge. It involves applying critical thinking and the scientific method to assess the validity of claims, demanding evidence, and remaining open to revising beliefs in light of new information. This chapter explores the concept of scientific skepticism, its key principles, its importance in various contexts, and its relationship to agnosticism.

What is Scientific Skepticism?

Scientific skepticism involves:

Questioning Claims: Approaching claims with a questioning attitude, demanding evidence, and not accepting assertions at face value.

Evidence-Based Reasoning: Relying on empirical evidence and logical reasoning to evaluate claims, rather than relying on authority, tradition, or intuition.

The Scientific Method: Applying the scientific method, which involves observation, hypothesis testing, experimentation, and peer review, to assess the validity of claims.

Falsifiability: Considering whether a claim is falsifiable, meaning that it can be tested and potentially disproven through observation or experimentation.

Occam's Razor: Preferring simpler explanations over more complex ones, when both can account for the available evidence.

Critical Thinking: Applying critical thinking skills, such as identifying logical fallacies, biases, and cognitive errors, to evaluate claims.

Key Principles of Scientific Skepticism:

Extraordinary Claims Require Extraordinary Evidence: The more extraordinary a claim is, the stronger the evidence required to support it.

Burden of Proof: The burden of proof lies with the person making a claim, not with the person questioning it.

Correlation Does Not Equal Causation: Just because two things are correlated does not mean that one causes the other.

Anecdotal Evidence is Not Reliable: Anecdotal evidence, based on personal experiences or isolated examples, is not reliable evidence for general claims.

Peer Review and Replication: Scientific findings should be subject to peer review and replication to ensure their validity.

Importance of Scientific Skepticism:

Scientific skepticism is crucial in various contexts:

Evaluating Scientific Claims: It helps to assess the validity of scientific claims and distinguish between sound science and pseudoscience.

Making Informed Decisions: It enables individuals to make informed decisions about their health, finances, and other aspects of their lives by evaluating evidence and avoiding scams and misinformation.

Promoting Critical Thinking: It encourages critical thinking skills, which are essential for navigating the complexities of the modern world and forming rational beliefs.

Combating Misinformation: It helps to identify and combat misinformation and disinformation, which can have harmful consequences.

Agnosticism and Scientific Skepticism:

Agnosticism strongly promotes scientific skepticism for several reasons:

Pursuit of Knowledge: Agnosticism emphasizes the importance of reason, evidence, and critical inquiry in the pursuit of knowledge. Scientific skepticism is a vital tool for evaluating claims and forming rational beliefs.

Rejection of Dogma: Agnosticism rejects dogma and fixed beliefs, encouraging open-mindedness and the questioning of authority. Scientific skepticism allows for the challenging of established ideas and the exploration of alternative explanations.

Limitations of Knowledge: Agnosticism recognizes the limitations of human knowledge and the potential for error. Scientific skepticism encourages humility and a willingness to revise beliefs in light of new evidence.

Evaluating Religious Claims: Agnostics often apply scientific skepticism to evaluate religious claims, demanding evidence and questioning supernatural explanations.

Developing Scientific Skepticism:

Scientific skepticism can be developed through:

Education and Training: Science education and critical thinking courses can help individuals develop scientific skepticism skills.

Reading and Research: Reading scientific literature and engaging in research can expose individuals to the process of scientific inquiry and the evaluation of evidence.

Skeptical Communities: Joining skeptical communities and engaging in discussions with other skeptics can help to sharpen critical thinking skills and expose individuals to different perspectives.

Practice and Application: Regularly applying scientific skepticism to evaluate claims in everyday life can strengthen these skills.

Scientific skepticism is a vital approach to evaluating claims and acquiring knowledge. It involves applying critical thinking and the scientific method to assess the validity of claims, demanding evidence, and remaining open to revising beliefs in light of new information. Agnosticism strongly promotes scientific skepticism, recognizing its importance for the pursuit of knowledge, the rejection of dogma, and the development of intellectual humility. By embracing scientific skepticism and cultivating these skills, we can become more informed, discerning, and responsible individuals, contributing to a more reasoned and enlightened society.

Chapter 46
Logical Fallacie

Logical fallacies are errors in reasoning that can undermine the validity of an argument. They can be persuasive and convincing on the surface, but they ultimately rely on flawed logic or irrelevant information. This chapter explores common logical fallacies, how to identify them, and their relevance to agnosticism and critical thinking.

What are Logical Fallacies?

Logical fallacies are flaws in reasoning that render an argument invalid. They can be intentional or unintentional, and they can be found in various contexts, from everyday conversations to political debates to academic discourse.

Types of Logical Fallacies:

Ad Hominem: Attacking the person making the argument rather than addressing the argument itself.

Example: "You can't trust anything he says about climate change because he's a politician."

Straw Man: Misrepresenting an opponent's argument to make it easier to attack.

Example: "My opponent wants to abolish the police. Clearly, they want to live in a lawless society."

Appeal to Authority: Claiming something is true simply because an authority figure says so, even if that figure is not an expert on the topic.

Example: "This celebrity endorses this weight loss product, so it must work."

False Dichotomy: Presenting two options as the only possibilities when in reality, there may be other options.

Example: "You're either with us or against us."

Bandwagon Fallacy: Claiming something is true because many people believe it.

Example: "Everyone knows that vaccines cause autism."

Appeal to Emotion: Using emotional appeals, such as fear or pity, to persuade rather than providing logical reasons.

Example: "If we don't increase military spending, we'll be vulnerable to attack."

Hasty Generalization: Drawing a conclusion based on insufficient evidence or a small sample size.

Example: "I met a rude teenager today, so all teenagers must be rude."

Correlation/Causation Fallacy: Assuming that because two things are correlated, one causes the other.

Example: "Ice cream sales increase in the summer, and so do crime rates. Therefore, ice cream causes crime."

Circular Reasoning: Using the conclusion of an argument as one of its premises.

Example: "The Bible is true because God wrote it, and we know God exists because the Bible says so."

Red Herring: Introducing an irrelevant topic to distract from the main issue.

Example: "You're criticizing my environmental policies, but what about all the jobs my opponent's plan will cost?"

Why are Logical Fallacies Important?

Understanding logical fallacies is important for several reasons:

Evaluating Arguments: It helps to identify flaws in reasoning and assess the validity of arguments.

Making Informed Decisions: It enables individuals to make informed decisions by recognizing manipulative or misleading arguments.

Improving Communication: It helps to construct sound arguments and communicate effectively.

Promoting Critical Thinking: It strengthens critical thinking skills and the ability to analyze information objectively.

Agnosticism and Logical Fallacies:

Agnosticism emphasizes the importance of critical thinking and evidence-based reasoning. Understanding logical fallacies is therefore crucial for agnostics in:

Evaluating Religious Claims: Agnostics often encounter arguments for religious beliefs that rely on logical fallacies. Recognizing these fallacies helps to assess the validity of such arguments.

Engaging in Debates: In debates about religion, philosophy, or other topics, being able to identify logical fallacies helps to construct sound arguments and counter flawed reasoning.

Promoting Rational Discourse: Agnostics can contribute to more rational and productive discussions by identifying and addressing logical fallacies in public discourse.

Identifying and Avoiding Logical Fallacies:

To identify logical fallacies, it is important to:

Pay attention to the structure of the argument: Look for flaws in the reasoning, irrelevant information, or emotional appeals.

Be aware of common fallacies: Familiarize yourself with the different types of logical fallacies and their characteristics.

Consider the context: The context of an argument can sometimes make it difficult to identify fallacies.

To avoid using logical fallacies in your own arguments:

Focus on the evidence and logic: Support your claims with evidence and sound reasoning.

Be charitable to your opponent: Accurately represent your opponent's arguments and avoid straw man fallacies.

Avoid emotional appeals: Focus on logical reasons and evidence rather than trying to manipulate emotions.

Logical fallacies are errors in reasoning that can undermine the validity of an argument. Understanding and identifying these fallacies is crucial for critical thinking, informed decision-making, and effective communication. Agnosticism emphasizes the importance of reason and evidence, making the recognition of logical fallacies essential for evaluating claims and engaging in rational discourse. By being mindful of logical fallacies and striving for sound reasoning, we can contribute to more productive and insightful discussions on a wide range of topics.

Chapter 47
The Scientific Method

The scientific method is a systematic approach to acquiring knowledge about the natural world. It involves a series of steps designed to ensure that our understanding of the world is based on empirical evidence, logical reasoning, and critical evaluation. This chapter explores the key elements of the scientific method, its importance in various fields, its limitations, and its relationship to agnosticism.

Steps of the Scientific Method:

Observation: The process begins with observing a phenomenon or asking a question about the natural world.

Hypothesis: Formulating a testable hypothesis, a proposed explanation for the observed phenomenon.

Prediction: Making predictions based on the hypothesis, outlining what should be observed if the hypothesis is true.

Experimentation: Designing and conducting experiments to test the predictions and gather data.

Analysis: Analyzing the data collected from the experiments to determine whether it supports or refutes the hypothesis.

Conclusion: Drawing conclusions based on the analysis of the data, either supporting or rejecting the hypothesis.

Communication: Communicating the findings to the scientific community through publications and presentations.

Key Elements of the Scientific Method:

Empirical Evidence: The scientific method relies on empirical evidence, meaning evidence that is based on observation or experimentation.

Testability: Scientific hypotheses must be testable, meaning that they can be supported or refuted through observation or experimentation.

Falsifiability: A scientific hypothesis must be falsifiable, meaning that it can be potentially disproven by evidence.

Replicability: Scientific experiments should be replicable, meaning that other scientists should be able to repeat the experiment and obtain similar results.

Peer Review: Scientific findings are typically subject to peer review, where other experts in the field evaluate the research for quality and validity.

Importance of the Scientific Method:

The scientific method is crucial in various fields:

Scientific Research: It is the foundation of scientific research, guiding the process of discovery and ensuring that scientific knowledge is based on evidence and rigorous testing.

Technology: It drives technological innovation, allowing for the development of new technologies based on scientific understanding.

Medicine: It is essential for developing new treatments and cures for diseases, ensuring that medical practices are based on evidence and research.

Environmental Science: It helps to understand environmental problems and develop solutions based on scientific evidence.

Social Sciences: It can be applied to study human behavior and social phenomena, although with some modifications to account for the complexities of human societies.

Limitations of the Scientific Method:

While the scientific method is a powerful tool for acquiring knowledge, it has limitations:

Subjectivity: While scientists strive for objectivity, some degree of subjectivity is inevitable in the interpretation of data and the formulation of hypotheses.

Ethical Considerations: The scientific method cannot address ethical or moral questions, which require philosophical and ethical reflection.

Complexity: Some phenomena, particularly those involving complex systems or human behavior, may be difficult to study using the traditional scientific method.

Paradigm Shifts: Scientific knowledge is not static but can undergo paradigm shifts, where fundamental assumptions and theories are revised in light of new evidence.

Agnosticism and the Scientific Method:

Agnosticism strongly supports the scientific method for several reasons:

Pursuit of Knowledge: Agnosticism emphasizes the importance of reason, evidence, and critical inquiry in the pursuit of knowledge. The scientific method is a vital tool for acquiring reliable knowledge about the natural world.

Rejection of Dogma: Agnosticism rejects dogma and fixed beliefs, encouraging open-mindedness and the questioning of authority. The scientific method allows for the challenging of established ideas and the exploration of alternative explanations.

Limitations of Knowledge: Agnosticism recognizes the limitations of human knowledge and the potential for error. The scientific method acknowledges the provisional nature of scientific knowledge and encourages a willingness to revise beliefs in light of new evidence.

Evaluating Supernatural Claims: Agnostics often apply the scientific method to evaluate supernatural claims, demanding evidence and seeking natural explanations for phenomena.

The scientific method is a systematic and rigorous approach to acquiring knowledge about the natural world. It involves a series of steps designed to ensure that our understanding of the world is based on empirical evidence, logical reasoning, and critical evaluation. Agnosticism strongly supports the scientific method, recognizing its importance for the pursuit of knowledge, the rejection of dogma, and the development of intellectual humility. By embracing the scientific method and cultivating its principles, we can gain a more reliable and nuanced understanding of the universe and our place within it.

Chapter 48
Rationality

Rationality is a cornerstone of human thought and action. It involves using reason and logic to form beliefs, make decisions, and solve problems. In a world often driven by emotions, biases, and misinformation, rationality provides a framework for clear thinking, sound judgment, and effective action. This chapter explores the concept of rationality, its different aspects, its importance in various contexts, and its relationship to agnosticism.

What is Rationality?

Rationality can be defined as the quality or state of being reasonable, based on facts or reason. It involves:

Logical Reasoning: Using logic and reason to draw inferences, evaluate arguments, and form conclusions.

Evidence-Based Thinking: Basing beliefs and decisions on evidence, rather than on emotions, intuition, or authority.

Critical Thinking: Applying critical thinking skills, such as analyzing information, evaluating evidence, and identifying biases, to form judgments.

Goal-Oriented Behavior: Acting in a way that is consistent with one's goals and values.

Adaptability: Being able to adapt one's beliefs and actions in response to new information or changing circumstances.

Aspects of Rationality:

Epistemic Rationality: This refers to forming beliefs that are consistent with the available evidence and using reason to update those beliefs in light of new information.

Instrumental Rationality: This involves choosing actions that are most likely to achieve one's goals, given the available information and resources.

Theoretical Rationality: This refers to the ability to understand and explain the world through reason and logic, seeking coherent and consistent explanations for phenomena.

Practical Rationality: This involves applying reason and logic to solve problems and make decisions in everyday life.

Importance of Rationality:

Rationality is crucial in various contexts:

Decision-Making: It enables individuals to make informed decisions based on evidence and logical reasoning, rather than being swayed by emotions or biases.

Problem-Solving: It helps to identify solutions to problems by analyzing the situation, evaluating options, and choosing the most effective course of action.

Scientific Inquiry: It is fundamental to the scientific method, guiding the process of observation, hypothesis testing, and experimentation.

Social Interaction: It promotes effective communication and understanding by encouraging individuals to express their ideas clearly and support them with reasons and evidence.

Personal Development: It allows individuals to live more fulfilling lives by making choices that are consistent with their values and goals.

Agnosticism and Rationality:

Agnosticism strongly promotes rationality for several reasons:

Pursuit of Knowledge: Agnosticism emphasizes the importance of reason, evidence, and critical inquiry in the pursuit of knowledge. Rationality is essential for evaluating claims, assessing evidence, and forming well-founded beliefs.

Rejection of Dogma: Agnosticism rejects dogma and fixed beliefs, encouraging open-mindedness and the questioning of authority. Rationality allows for the challenging of established ideas and the exploration of alternative perspectives.

Skepticism and Doubt: Agnosticism embraces skepticism and doubt as tools for uncovering the truth. Rationality helps to identify biases, logical fallacies, and potential flaws in arguments.

Intellectual Humility: Agnosticism promotes intellectual humility, recognizing the limitations of human knowledge and the potential for error. Rationality encourages self-reflection and a willingness to revise beliefs in light of new evidence.

Challenges to Rationality:

Rationality faces challenges from various sources:

Cognitive Biases: Humans are prone to cognitive biases, mental shortcuts that can distort our thinking and lead to irrational decisions.

Emotional Influences: Emotions can cloud our judgment and lead to irrational behavior.

Social Pressures: Social pressures and conformity can lead individuals to adopt beliefs or engage in actions that are not rational.

Misinformation: The spread of misinformation and disinformation can make it difficult to distinguish between truth and falsehood, hindering rational decision-making.

Rationality is a cornerstone of human thought and action, enabling us to make informed decisions, solve problems, and understand the world around us. Agnosticism strongly promotes rationality, recognizing its importance for the pursuit of knowledge, the rejection of dogma, and the development of intellectual humility. By embracing rationality and cultivating critical thinking skills, we can overcome the challenges to rational thought and strive to live more fulfilling and meaningful lives.

Chapter 49
Emotions and Reason

Emotions and reason are often perceived as opposing forces, with emotions seen as irrational and disruptive to logical thinking. However, the relationship between emotions and reason is far more complex and intertwined. Emotions play a vital role in human cognition, influencing our perceptions, judgments, and decisions. This chapter explores the interplay between emotions and reason, examining how emotions influence our thinking, the importance of emotional intelligence, and how agnosticism views the role of emotions in a rational life.

The Nature of Emotions:

Emotions are complex psychological states that involve subjective feelings, physiological responses, and behavioral expressions. They can be triggered by internal or external stimuli and can range in intensity from mild to intense.

Functions of Emotions:

Emotions serve several important functions:

Motivation: Emotions can motivate us to act, driving us towards goals or away from threats. For example, fear can motivate us to avoid danger, while joy can motivate us to pursue pleasurable experiences.

Social Communication: Emotions help us to communicate with others, expressing our feelings and intentions. Facial expressions, body language, and tone of voice convey emotional information that can influence social interactions.

Decision-Making: Emotions can influence our decisions, guiding us towards choices that feel right or avoiding those that feel wrong.

Learning and Memory: Emotions can enhance learning and memory, making emotionally charged events more memorable.

How Emotions Influence Reasoning:

Emotions can influence our reasoning in various ways:

Attention and Perception: Emotions can direct our attention towards certain stimuli and influence how we perceive the world. For example, when we are feeling anxious, we may be more likely to perceive threats in our environment.

Judgment and Decision-Making: Emotions can bias our judgments and decisions, leading us to favor options that feel good or avoid those that feel bad, even if those choices are not logically optimal.

Memory and Recall: Emotions can influence our memory and recall, making emotionally charged events more salient and accessible.

Cognitive Control: Strong emotions can impair cognitive control, making it difficult to focus, think clearly, and make rational decisions.

Emotional Intelligence:

Emotional intelligence is the ability to understand and manage one's own emotions and the emotions of others. It involves:

Self-Awareness: Recognizing and understanding one's own emotions.

Self-Regulation: Managing one's emotions effectively.

Motivation: Using emotions to motivate oneself and others.

Empathy: Understanding and sharing the emotions of others.

Social Skills: Building and maintaining positive relationships.

Agnosticism and the Role of Emotions:

Agnosticism acknowledges the importance of emotions in human life while emphasizing the importance of reason and critical thinking. Agnostics may:

Recognize the Influence of Emotions: They understand that emotions can influence their thinking and decision-making, and they strive to be aware of these influences.

Cultivate Emotional Intelligence: They may seek to develop emotional intelligence to better understand and manage their emotions and the emotions of others.

Balance Emotions and Reason: They strive to balance emotions and reason, using emotions to inform their decisions but not letting emotions override logic and evidence.

Promote Empathy and Compassion: They value empathy and compassion as important human qualities that can guide ethical behavior and social interactions.

Emotions and reason are not opposing forces but rather intertwined aspects of human cognition. Emotions play a vital role in motivation, social communication, decision-making, and learning. While emotions can influence our reasoning in various ways, emotional intelligence can help us to understand and manage our emotions effectively. Agnosticism recognizes the importance of emotions in human life while emphasizing the importance of reason and critical thinking. By cultivating emotional intelligence and striving for a balance between emotions and reason, we can live more fulfilling and meaningful lives.

Chapter 50
Cognitive Biases

Cognitive biases are systematic errors in thinking that can affect our judgments and decisions. They are mental shortcuts that our brains use to process information quickly, but they can sometimes lead to irrational or inaccurate conclusions. This chapter explores various cognitive biases, their impact on our beliefs and behaviors, and how understanding these biases can help us to think more critically and make better decisions.

What are Cognitive Biases?

Cognitive biases are systematic patterns of deviation from norm or rationality in judgment. They are often a result of our brain's attempt to simplify complex situations and make quick decisions, but they can lead to flawed thinking and inaccurate perceptions.

Common Cognitive Biases:

Confirmation Bias: The tendency to seek out and interpret information that confirms our existing beliefs, while ignoring or dismissing information that contradicts them.

Example: A person who believes in astrology may only remember the times when their horoscope was accurate and forget the times when it was not.

Anchoring Bias: The tendency to rely too heavily on the first piece of information we receive on a topic, even if that information is irrelevant or inaccurate.

Example: A salesperson might start with a high price for a product, making a lower offer seem more appealing even if it is still overpriced.

Availability Heuristic: The tendency to overestimate the likelihood of events that are easily recalled, often because they are vivid or recent.

Example: After seeing a news report about a plane crash, people may overestimate the likelihood of plane crashes and become more afraid of flying.

Dunning-Kruger Effect: The tendency for people with low ability in a particular area to overestimate their ability, while people with high ability tend to underestimate their ability.

Example: A person who is a poor public speaker may believe they are a great speaker, while a skilled speaker may be overly critical of their performance.

Halo Effect: The tendency to judge someone based on a single positive trait or characteristic.

Example: A person who is physically attractive may be perceived as being more intelligent or trustworthy.

In-Group Bias: The tendency to favor members of our own group over outsiders.

Example: People may be more likely to hire or promote someone from their own ethnic group or social circle.

Loss Aversion: The tendency to feel the pain of a loss more strongly than the pleasure of an equivalent gain.

Example: People may be more reluctant to sell a stock at a loss, even if it is the rational thing to do.

Overconfidence Bias: The tendency to overestimate our own abilities and knowledge.

Example: A student may overestimate their ability to perform well on an exam and not study sufficiently.

Status Quo Bias: The tendency to prefer the current state of affairs, even if there are better alternatives.

Example: People may be reluctant to switch to a new phone or internet provider, even if the new provider offers better service or lower prices.

Impact of Cognitive Biases:

Cognitive biases can have a significant impact on our beliefs, behaviors, and decisions:

Reinforcing Prejudices: Biases can reinforce prejudices and stereotypes, leading to discrimination and unfair treatment.

Distorting Judgments: Biases can distort our judgments and lead to inaccurate assessments of situations and people.

Hindering Decision-Making: Biases can hinder rational decision-making, leading to poor choices and undesirable outcomes.

Impeding Learning: Biases can impede learning by making it difficult to consider alternative perspectives and revise our beliefs.

Agnosticism and Cognitive Biases:

Agnosticism emphasizes the importance of critical thinking and self-reflection. Understanding cognitive biases is therefore crucial for agnostics in:

Identifying Biases in Oneself: Agnostics strive to be aware of their own biases and how they might influence their thinking.

Evaluating Information Critically: Recognizing cognitive biases helps to evaluate information critically and avoid being swayed by flawed reasoning or misleading information.

Making Informed Decisions: Understanding biases can help to make more informed and rational decisions by mitigating the influence of these mental shortcuts.

Promoting Open-Mindedness: Awareness of cognitive biases encourages open-mindedness and a willingness to consider alternative perspectives.

Overcoming Cognitive Biases:

While it is impossible to eliminate cognitive biases entirely, there are strategies for mitigating their influence:

Awareness: Becoming aware of common biases and how they operate is the first step towards overcoming them.

Critical Thinking: Applying critical thinking skills, such as seeking out diverse perspectives, evaluating evidence carefully, and questioning assumptions, can help to reduce the impact of biases.

Self-Reflection: Engaging in self-reflection and seeking feedback from others can help to identify and address personal biases.

Deliberate Decision-Making: Taking time to make deliberate and conscious decisions, rather than relying on intuition or quick judgments, can help to mitigate the influence of biases.

Cognitive biases are systematic errors in thinking that can affect our judgments and decisions. Understanding these biases is crucial for critical thinking, informed decision-making, and personal development. Agnosticism emphasizes the importance of reason and self-reflection, making the recognition of cognitive biases essential for evaluating information and forming rational beliefs. By being mindful of cognitive biases and employing strategies to mitigate their influence, we can strive to think more clearly, make better decisions, and live more fulfilling lives.

Chapter 51
The Agnostic Community

While agnosticism is often seen as an individual philosophical stance, it also encompasses a vibrant and growing community of individuals who share a commitment to reason, evidence, and open-minded inquiry. This chapter explores the agnostic community, its diverse forms, the benefits of connecting with other agnostics, and the ways in which agnostics can engage with and contribute to this community.

The Diversity of the Agnostic Community:

The agnostic community is diverse, encompassing individuals from various backgrounds, cultures, and walks of life. Agnostics may hold different beliefs about the existence of God, the nature of reality, and the meaning of life. However, they share a common commitment to:

Reason and Evidence: Agnostics value reason and evidence as the primary tools for understanding the world and forming beliefs.

Critical Thinking: They encourage critical thinking and skepticism, questioning assumptions and demanding evidence for claims.

Open-Mindedness: They are open to considering different perspectives and revising their beliefs in light of new information.

Intellectual Humility: They recognize the limitations of human knowledge and the potential for error.

Ethical Values: They often share a commitment to ethical values, such as compassion, fairness, and justice.

Forms of Agnostic Community:

Online Communities: Online forums, social media groups, and websites provide spaces for agnostics to connect with each other, share ideas, and engage in discussions.

Local Groups and Meetups: Many cities and towns have local agnostic groups that organize meetings, events, and social gatherings.

Conferences and Workshops: Agnostic organizations and groups often host conferences and workshops where agnostics can learn from experts, engage in discussions, and connect with other like-minded individuals.

Secular Humanist Organizations: Many agnostics are also involved in secular humanist organizations, which promote reason, ethics, and human values.

Benefits of Connecting with Other Agnostics:

Connecting with other agnostics can provide numerous benefits:

Sense of Belonging: It can create a sense of belonging and community for individuals who may feel isolated or marginalized in predominantly religious societies.

Intellectual Stimulation: It provides opportunities for intellectual stimulation and engagement with diverse perspectives on philosophical, scientific, and social issues.

Support and Encouragement: It offers support and encouragement for individuals navigating the challenges of living an agnostic life in a world often shaped by religious beliefs.

Social Connection: It creates opportunities for social connection and friendships with like-minded individuals.

Collective Action: It can facilitate collective action and advocacy for secular values and causes, such as the separation of church and state and the promotion of critical thinking in education.

Engaging with the Agnostic Community:

Agnostics can engage with the community in various ways:

Participating in Online Forums: Joining online forums and social media groups to share ideas, ask questions, and engage in discussions.

Attending Local Meetups: Attending local agnostic group meetings and events to connect with other agnostics in their area.

Volunteering for Agnostic Organizations: Volunteering time and skills to support agnostic organizations and their efforts to promote secular values and education.

Attending Conferences and Workshops: Participating in conferences and workshops to learn from experts and engage with other agnostics on a deeper level.

Creating Content: Creating and sharing content, such as blog posts, articles, or videos, that promotes agnostic perspectives and contributes to the community's knowledge base.

The agnostic community is a vibrant and growing network of individuals who share a commitment to reason, evidence, and open-minded inquiry. It provides a sense of belonging, intellectual stimulation, support, and opportunities for social connection and collective action. By engaging with the agnostic community, individuals can connect with like-minded individuals, learn from others, and contribute to the promotion of secular values and critical thinking in society. As the agnostic community continues to grow and evolve, it plays an increasingly important role in fostering a more rational, tolerant, and inclusive world.

Chapter 52
Resources for Agnostics

In a world where religious information and institutions are readily available, finding resources specifically tailored for agnostics can sometimes be challenging. This chapter aims to provide a comprehensive guide to resources that can help agnostics deepen their understanding of agnosticism, connect with the agnostic community, and navigate the complexities of living an agnostic life.

Types of Resources:

Books: Books offer in-depth explorations of agnosticism, its philosophical foundations, and its implications for various aspects of life.

Articles and Websites: Articles and websites provide accessible and up-to-date information on agnosticism, current debates, and relevant news.

Podcasts and Videos: Podcasts and videos offer engaging and convenient ways to learn about agnosticism, hear from experts, and explore different perspectives.

Organizations and Communities: Agnostic organizations and communities provide opportunities to connect with other agnostics, participate in events, and access support and resources.

Secular Humanist Resources: Many secular humanist resources are also relevant to agnostics, as they share common values and concerns.

Books:
Classic Works:

"The Varieties of Religious Experience" by William James: Explores the psychology of religious experience from a philosophical perspective.

"Why I Am Not a Christian" by Bertrand Russell: A classic essay outlining Russell's reasons for rejecting Christianity and embracing agnosticism.

"The God Delusion" by Richard Dawkins: A critique of religion and a defense of atheism, with arguments that may resonate with agnostics.

Contemporary Works:

"The Moral Landscape: How Science Can Determine Human Values" by Sam Harris: Argues that science can inform our understanding of morality and human values.

"Waking Up: A Guide to Spirituality Without Religion" by Sam Harris: Explores the nature of consciousness and spirituality from a secular perspective.

"God: The Failed Hypothesis. How Science Shows That God Does Not Exist" by Victor J. Stenger: Presents scientific arguments against the existence of God.

"A Manual for Creating Atheists" by Peter Boghossian: Provides tools and techniques for engaging in critical thinking and questioning religious beliefs.

Articles and Websites:

The Secular Web: A comprehensive online resource for agnosticism, atheism, and secular humanism, with articles, essays, and forums.

American Humanist Association: The website of the American Humanist Association offers information on secular humanism, agnosticism, and related topics.

The Humanist: A magazine published by the American Humanist Association, covering a wide range of topics related to secularism, humanism, and agnosticism.

Skeptic Magazine: A magazine that promotes scientific skepticism and critical thinking, with articles on various topics, including religion and pseudoscience.

Center for Inquiry: A non-profit organization that promotes science, reason, and secular values, with resources on agnosticism and related topics.

Podcasts and Videos:

The Atheist Experience: A live call-in show where hosts discuss atheism, agnosticism, and religion with callers.

The Thinking Atheist: A podcast that explores atheism, skepticism, and critical thinking.

Secular Talk Radio: A radio show and podcast that covers secularism, humanism, and atheism.

The Friendly Atheist Podcast: A podcast that discusses atheism, religion, and secularism.

YouTube Channels: Numerous YouTube channels offer content on agnosticism, atheism, skepticism, and secular humanism.

Organizations and Communities:

American Atheists: A national organization that advocates for atheists and promotes the separation of church and state.

Freedom From Religion Foundation: A non-profit organization that works to protect the separation of church and state and educate the public about atheism and agnosticism.

Center for Inquiry: A non-profit organization that promotes science, reason, and secular values through education, research, and advocacy.

Local Agnostic Groups: Many cities and towns have local agnostic groups that organize meetings, events, and social gatherings.

Secular Humanist Resources:

Council for Secular Humanism: A non-profit organization that promotes secular humanism and provides resources on ethics, philosophy, and science.

International Humanist and Ethical Union: A global organization that unites humanist and ethical organizations around the world.

The Humanist Manifesto: A document that outlines the principles of secular humanism.

Agnostics have a wealth of resources available to them, from books and articles to podcasts and online communities. These resources can help agnostics deepen their understanding of agnosticism, connect with the agnostic community, and navigate the complexities of living an agnostic life. By utilizing these resources, agnostics can strengthen their critical thinking skills, expand their knowledge, and find support and encouragement in their journey of inquiry and self-discovery.

Chapter 53
Living as an Agnostic

Living as an agnostic is an ongoing journey of exploration, critical thinking, and ethical living. It involves embracing uncertainty, seeking knowledge, and finding meaning and purpose in a world without absolute certainty or divine guidance. This chapter explores the practical aspects of living as an agnostic, offering guidance on navigating various challenges, building a meaningful life, and contributing to a better world.

Embracing Uncertainty:

Agnosticism acknowledges the limitations of human knowledge and the inherent uncertainty of the universe. Living as an agnostic involves embracing this uncertainty, accepting that some questions may not have definitive answers, and finding comfort in the unknown.

Letting Go of the Need for Certainty: It involves letting go of the need for absolute certainty and embracing the possibility that our understanding of the world may always be incomplete.

Finding Beauty in the Mystery: It means appreciating the mystery and wonder of the universe, finding beauty in the unknown, and embracing the ongoing quest for knowledge.

Living with Openness: It involves living with an open mind, being willing to consider different perspectives, and revising beliefs in light of new evidence.

Seeking Knowledge and Understanding:

Agnosticism encourages a lifelong pursuit of knowledge and understanding. It involves actively seeking out information, engaging in critical thinking, and exploring different perspectives.

Cultivating Curiosity: It means cultivating curiosity about the world, asking questions, and seeking answers through reason and evidence.

Engaging with Science: It involves engaging with science, appreciating its ability to provide natural explanations for phenomena, and recognizing its limitations.

Exploring Philosophy: It means exploring philosophy, engaging with different philosophical perspectives, and developing one's own worldview.

Learning from Others: It involves learning from others, engaging in dialogue and debate, and being open to different viewpoints.

Finding Meaning and Purpose:

In the absence of a predetermined purpose or divine plan, agnostics create their own meaning and purpose in life. This can involve:

Personal Values: Identifying and living in accordance with one's personal values, such as compassion, integrity, and justice.

Relationships: Building meaningful relationships with family, friends, and community.

Contribution: Contributing to something larger than oneself, whether through work, volunteering, or activism.

Creativity: Expressing oneself through creative pursuits, such as art, music, writing, or other forms of self-expression.

Personal Growth: Striving for personal growth and self-improvement, developing one's talents and abilities, and pursuing lifelong learning.

Navigating Challenges:

Living as an agnostic can present challenges in a world often shaped by religious beliefs:

Social Pressure: Agnostics may face social pressure to conform to religious norms or may be excluded from certain social circles or events.

Family and Relationships: Agnostic beliefs may differ from those of family members or loved ones, leading to potential conflicts or misunderstandings.

Existential Questions: Agnosticism may raise existential questions about the meaning of life, the nature of consciousness, and the possibility of an afterlife.

Moral Dilemmas: Agnostics may face moral dilemmas that require careful consideration and may not have easy answers.

Strategies for Living as an Agnostic:

Building a Support Network: Connecting with other agnostics and building a support network can provide a sense of community and belonging.

Communicating Effectively: Communicating openly and respectfully with family and friends about agnostic beliefs can help to foster understanding and avoid conflict.

Engaging in Self-Reflection: Engaging in self-reflection and exploring philosophical and existential questions can help to develop a deeper understanding of oneself and one's place in the world.

Living Ethically: Living ethically and contributing to the greater good can provide a sense of purpose and fulfillment.

Seeking Professional Support: If needed, seeking professional support from therapists or counselors can help to navigate challenges and address existential or emotional concerns.

Living as an agnostic is an ongoing journey of exploration, critical thinking, and ethical living. It involves embracing uncertainty, seeking knowledge, finding meaning and purpose, and navigating challenges with courage and resilience. By cultivating intellectual curiosity, embracing human values, and contributing to a better world, agnostics can live fulfilling and meaningful lives, even in the absence of absolute certainty or divine guidance.

Chapter 54
Finding Meaning

One of the common challenges for those embracing an agnostic worldview is the question of meaning. If there is no predetermined purpose or divine plan, how do we find meaning and purpose in life? This chapter explores the various ways agnostics can find meaning, drawing on human values, relationships, creativity, and the pursuit of knowledge and self-discovery.

Meaning in a World Without Certainty:
The agnostic perspective acknowledges the absence of absolute certainty and the lack of a predetermined purpose. This can be liberating but also challenging, as it requires individuals to actively create their own meaning and purpose.

Sources of Meaning:
Agnostics can find meaning in various aspects of life:

Human Values: Living in accordance with one's values, such as compassion, integrity, justice, and kindness, can provide a sense of purpose and direction.

Relationships: Building and nurturing meaningful relationships with family, friends, and community can provide a sense of belonging, love, and connection.

Contribution: Contributing to something larger than oneself, whether through work, volunteering, activism, or creative endeavors, can create a sense of purpose and fulfillment.

Creativity: Expressing oneself through creative pursuits, such as art, music, writing, or other forms of self-expression, can bring joy, fulfillment, and a sense of accomplishment.

Knowledge and Learning: Pursuing knowledge, learning new skills, and exploring different perspectives can provide intellectual stimulation and a sense of growth and discovery.

Nature and the Universe: Appreciating the beauty and complexity of the natural world and the universe can evoke a sense of awe, wonder, and connection to something larger than oneself.

Personal Growth: Striving for personal growth and self-improvement, developing one's talents and abilities, and pursuing self-discovery can provide a sense of direction and purpose.

Creating Meaning:

Finding meaning is an active process that involves:

Self-Reflection: Reflecting on one's values, passions, and interests to identify what is truly meaningful.

Setting Goals: Setting goals and pursuing them with purpose and intention.

Engaging with the World: Actively engaging with the world, seeking out new experiences, and connecting with others.

Finding Joy in the Everyday: Appreciating the small things in life, finding joy in everyday moments, and cultivating gratitude.

Meaning and the Human Condition:

The search for meaning is a fundamental aspect of the human condition. Agnosticism recognizes that meaning is not something imposed from the outside but rather something we create through our choices, actions, and relationships.

Challenges and Opportunities:

Existential Angst: The absence of a predetermined purpose can lead to existential angst and questions about the meaning of life.

Nihilism: Some may struggle with nihilism, the belief that life is inherently meaningless.

Finding Purpose: Identifying and pursuing meaningful goals and activities can be challenging.

However, agnosticism also offers opportunities for finding meaning:

Freedom and Autonomy: The absence of a predetermined purpose gives individuals the freedom and autonomy to create their own meaning.

Diverse Sources of Meaning: Agnostics can draw on a wide range of sources to find meaning, from human values and relationships to creativity and the pursuit of knowledge.

Meaning in the Journey: Agnosticism encourages finding meaning in the journey of life itself, appreciating the present moment and embracing the ongoing quest for knowledge and self-discovery.

Conclusion:

Finding meaning in a world without certainty is a challenge and an opportunity. Agnosticism encourages individuals to actively create their own meaning, drawing on human values, relationships, creativity, and the pursuit of knowledge and self-discovery. By embracing the freedom and autonomy that comes with an agnostic worldview, individuals can find purpose and fulfillment in their lives, even in the absence of a predetermined plan or divine guidance.

Chapter 55
Celebrating Life

Agnosticism, with its embrace of reason, uncertainty, and the natural world, offers a unique perspective on celebrating life. Free from the constraints of dogma and supernatural beliefs, agnostics can find joy and wonder in the everyday, appreciate the beauty and complexity of the universe, and cherish the preciousness of human existence. This chapter explores how agnostics can celebrate life, finding fulfillment in relationships, creativity, and the pursuit of knowledge and personal growth.

Celebrating the Human Experience:

Agnosticism recognizes the value and uniqueness of human existence. It encourages us to celebrate:

Consciousness and Awareness: Our ability to experience the world, to think, to feel, and to connect with others is a remarkable gift.

Reason and Creativity: Our capacity for reason, creativity, and innovation allows us to explore the universe, create art, and build a better future.

Love and Connection: Our ability to form deep and meaningful relationships with others brings joy, support, and a sense of belonging.

The Natural World: The beauty, complexity, and diversity of the natural world offer endless opportunities for wonder, exploration, and appreciation.

Finding Joy in the Everyday:

Agnostics can find joy and meaning in the everyday moments of life:

Simple Pleasures: Savoring the simple pleasures of life, such as a good meal, a beautiful sunset, or a meaningful conversation.

Gratitude: Cultivating gratitude for the good things in life, both big and small.

Mindfulness: Practicing mindfulness, paying attention to the present moment, and appreciating the richness of experience.

Connection with Nature: Spending time in nature, connecting with the natural world, and finding peace and tranquility.

Celebrating Relationships:

Relationships are a vital source of meaning and joy for agnostics. Celebrating relationships involves:

Nurturing Connections: Nurturing and strengthening connections with family, friends, and loved ones.

Expressing Appreciation: Expressing appreciation for the people in our lives and showing them how much we care.

Building Community: Building community and connecting with others who share our values and interests.

Sharing Experiences: Sharing experiences, creating memories, and celebrating milestones with loved ones.

Celebrating Creativity:

Creativity is a powerful way to express oneself, find fulfillment, and connect with others. Agnostics can celebrate creativity through:

Artistic Expression: Engaging in artistic pursuits, such as painting, music, writing, or dance.

Innovation and Invention: Exploring new ideas, developing innovative solutions, and contributing to progress in various fields.

Self-Expression: Finding ways to express oneself authentically, whether through art, writing, music, or other creative outlets.

Appreciating Art and Culture: Enjoying and appreciating the art, music, literature, and other cultural expressions of humanity.

Celebrating Knowledge and Growth:
The pursuit of knowledge and personal growth is a lifelong journey for agnostics. Celebrating knowledge involves:

Lifelong Learning: Engaging in lifelong learning, exploring new subjects, and expanding one's understanding of the world.

Intellectual Curiosity: Cultivating intellectual curiosity, asking questions, and seeking answers through reason and evidence.

Personal Growth: Striving for personal growth and self-improvement, developing one's talents and abilities, and pursuing self-discovery.

Sharing Knowledge: Sharing knowledge and insights with others, contributing to education and intellectual discourse.

Conclusion:
Agnosticism offers a unique perspective on celebrating life, free from the constraints of dogma and supernatural beliefs. Agnostics can find joy and wonder in the everyday, appreciate the beauty and complexity of the universe, and cherish the preciousness of human existence. By celebrating relationships, creativity, and the pursuit of knowledge and personal growth, agnostics can live fulfilling and meaningful lives, embracing the richness and diversity of human experience.

Chapter 56
The Future of Agnosticism

Agnosticism, with its emphasis on reason, evidence, and open-minded inquiry, is poised to play an increasingly important role in a world grappling with rapid technological advancements, social and political changes, and the decline of traditional religious beliefs. This chapter explores the future of agnosticism, considering its potential impact on society, the challenges it may face, and the opportunities it has to contribute to a more rational, tolerant, and progressive world.

Trends Shaping the Future of Agnosticism:
Several trends are shaping the future of agnosticism:

Rise of Secularism: The number of people identifying as non-religious is growing globally, creating a more receptive environment for agnostic perspectives.

Scientific Progress: Continued advancements in science and technology are providing natural explanations for phenomena once attributed to supernatural causes, further supporting a naturalistic worldview.

Information Age: The internet and social media provide platforms for agnostics to connect, share ideas, and engage in public discourse.

Globalization and Cultural Exchange: Increased globalization and cultural exchange expose people to diverse beliefs and perspectives, challenging traditional religious dogmas and promoting greater understanding.

Social and Political Changes: Social and political movements advocating for human rights, equality, and social justice often align with agnostic values, creating opportunities for collaboration and shared action.

Potential Impact of Agnosticism:

Agnosticism has the potential to influence various aspects of society:

Education: Promoting critical thinking, scientific inquiry, and secular education can foster a more informed and rational citizenry.

Politics and Governance: Advocating for secular governance, evidence-based policymaking, and the separation of church and state can contribute to a more just and equitable society.

Ethics and Morality: Offering a secular and humanistic framework for ethical decision-making can guide individuals and societies towards more compassionate and responsible behavior.

Science and Technology: Encouraging scientific literacy and responsible innovation can help to harness the benefits of technology while mitigating its risks.

Interfaith Dialogue: Promoting dialogue and understanding between people of different faiths and none can foster greater tolerance and cooperation.

Challenges and Opportunities:

Agnosticism faces several challenges in the future:

Religious Resistance: Religious institutions and individuals may resist the growing influence of agnosticism, leading to potential conflict and backlash.

Misconceptions and Stereotypes: Agnosticism may continue to be misunderstood or misrepresented, requiring ongoing efforts to educate the public and promote accurate understanding.

Anti-Intellectualism: The rise of anti-intellectualism and the rejection of expertise can pose challenges to the agnostic emphasis on reason and evidence.

However, agnosticism also has significant opportunities:

Growing Secularism: The growing number of non-religious individuals creates a receptive audience for agnostic perspectives and values.

Technological Advancements: The internet and social media provide platforms for agnostics to connect, organize, and amplify their voices.

Collaboration with Allies: Agnostics can collaborate with allies in the secular humanist, scientific, and social justice communities to promote shared goals and values.

The Role of the Agnostic Community:

The agnostic community has a crucial role to play in shaping the future of agnosticism:

Education and Outreach: Educating the public about agnosticism, its principles, and its contributions to society.

Community Building: Creating welcoming and inclusive spaces for agnostics to connect, support each other, and engage in meaningful discussions.

Advocacy: Advocating for secular values, such as the separation of church and state, freedom of thought and expression, and science-based education.

Dialogue and Collaboration: Engaging in dialogue and collaboration with people of other faiths and none to promote understanding and cooperation.

The future of agnosticism is bright, with opportunities to influence society, promote reason and critical thinking, and contribute to a more tolerant and progressive world. By embracing the challenges and seizing the opportunities, agnostics can play a vital role in shaping a future where human values, scientific inquiry, and open-minded dialogue guide our path towards a more fulfilling and sustainable future for all.

Epilogue

You have reached the end of this book, but unlike what we often expect upon finishing a work, this is not the conclusion of a journey. It is merely the beginning of a new way of seeing, thinking, and questioning. Throughout these pages, you have been guided to confront the vastness of the unknown, challenge comfortable certainties, and embrace intellectual humility as an essential virtue.

Agnosticism, as explored here, is not merely a philosophy; it is a way of being in the world. It is the courage to embrace doubt without fear and the capacity to accept that the unknown is not an enemy to be vanquished but a mystery to be respected. By questioning the limits of what we can know, you have freed yourself from the traps of dogmatism and the arrogance of absolute knowledge.

The world around you may seem unchanged, but now, perhaps, you see it with new eyes. Every certainty that once seemed unshakable now carries within it the seed of inquiry; every belief is subject to examination, and every answer raises new questions. This is the mark of a transformed mind: the refusal to settle into intellectual comfort.

Along the way, you were invited to ponder fundamental questions about knowledge, faith, and the unknown. But more than the answers—or the lack thereof—the value lies in the process. You have recognized that by adopting the agnostic stance, you are affirming something essentially human: that we do not need absolute certainties to live meaningful lives and to seek understanding.

If there is one takeaway from this book, let it be the awareness that doubt is not a failure. On the contrary, it is the foundation upon which true critical thinking, insatiable curiosity, and the ability to grow are built. Doubt liberates us, for it allows us to explore ideas without the constraints of fearing we might be wrong.

And now? What will you do with this knowledge, with the tools of thought you have gained? Perhaps you will apply this perspective to how you understand the universe, human relationships, or even the questions of everyday life. Perhaps, more than ever, you will choose to listen attentively to those with beliefs different from your own—not to refute them but to learn from them, recognizing the infinite complexity of human experience.

Agnosticism, as you have seen, does not require you to be skeptical of everything or to abandon your deepest convictions. It does, however, invite you to maintain a spirit of constant inquiry, a critical perspective, and a willingness to reconsider. After all, it is in the dialogue between ideas, in the interplay between the known and the unknown, that humanity finds its greatest potential.

If this book has sparked anything within you, let it be the willingness to continue exploring. May the questions that formed here be the beginning of new journeys, may your quest for understanding lead you to even broader horizons, and may you never lose the drive to ask, "What if?"

To conclude a book like this is not to end a journey but to begin another. The universe is vast, knowledge is infinite, and our capacity to learn and grow never ceases. So, continue walking, for true knowledge is not a destination but a path—and it is always ahead, waiting to be discovered.

Thank you for embarking on this journey. May the spirit of doubt, curiosity, and humility guide your next steps.

www.ingramcontent.com/pod-product-compliance
Lightning Source LLC
LaVergne TN
LVHW040056080526
838202LV00045B/3655